WITHDRAWN

The HARVARD GUIDE to CAREERS

FIFTH EDITION

**MARTHA P. LEAPE and
SUSAN M. VACCA**
Office of Career Services
Faculty of Arts and Sciences
Harvard University
Cambridge, Massachusetts
1995

D1115444

© 1982, 1983, 1987, 1991, 1995 by the President and Fellows of Harvard College
All rights reserved
Printed in the United States of America
01 00 99 98 97 96 95   10 9 8 7 6 5 4 3 2 1

Library of Congress Cataloging-in-Publication Data

Leape, Martha P.
    The Harvard guide to careers / Martha P. Leape and Susan M. Vacca.
— 5th ed.
        p.   cm.
    Includes bibliographical references and index.
    ISBN 0-943747-16-3 (pbk.)
    1. Vocational guidance—United States. 2. Job hunting—United
States. 3. Vocational guidance—United States—Bibliography.
4. Vocational guidance—Information services—United States.
I. Vacca, Susan M., 1954-   . II. Title.
HF5382.5.U5L36 1995
331.7'02--dc20   95-23202
                                                         CIP

Contents

6. CAREER DEVELOPMENT SKILLS

Preface

The fifth edition of *The Harvard Guide to Careers* addresses the changing nature of work and careers. To assist you in preparing for a world in which you must assume increasing responsibility for your professional growth, this guide discusses issues you are likely to encounter in your career development.

Our goal, as has been the case with previous editions, has been to introduce the various phases of career exploration and decision making and to teach the necessary skills. To this end, we have included discussions on learning about yourself, researching careers and work opportunities, conducting a job hunt, making a successful transition to a new job, keeping your finances on an even keel, and planning the next step.

We hope that we have conveyed the sense of adventure and excitement that we both feel whenever we talk to individuals about their career development.

NOTE: The pronouns "he," "him," and "his" are used throughout the book to denote a person of either gender. We are involved in serving the career development needs of both women and men, and this book is intended to speak to all.

We wish to thank Karen From for her valuable insights and thoughtful advice in the editing of this manuscript. We also appreciate her meticulous attention to detail in the design and production of this book.

Thanks are also due to Karin Powell for her assistance in the preparation of sample resumes and letters and for proofreading the manuscript. Thanks also to Paul Bohlmann for designing the cover. Finally, we wish to thank all of our colleagues at the Office of Career Services for their continuing advice and support.

M.P.L.
S.M.V.

Chapter 1

THE CHANGING NATURE
OF CAREERS

INTRODUCTION

A generation ago talented young people who went to work for large companies could expect to spend their entire careers with their first employers. If they performed well, worked hard, and were loyal to their organization, they would be rewarded with promotion to more important positions and with salary increases. The career ladder was clear, and as long as the employee met the performance expectations of his employer, he could count on steady advancement in the management structure.

During this era, the choice of a first employer was very important. Deciding to go with IBM was like joining a family. As the older managers retired, or the company expanded, the younger employees were moved up the management hierarchy. The acceptance of an entry management position in a large corporation was a decision that programmed an entire career.

All that has changed in the last few years. A host of forces have conspired to require corporations to radically change the way that they conduct their business. The rapidly developing global marketplace provides great opportunity and generates intense competition. Work moves to where it can be accomplished most economically; markets grow and diminish in response to socioeconomic forces worldwide. Technological advances in information systems and communication also change how and by whom work can be done, causing both the loss of jobs and the development of new, different jobs.

To be able to respond quickly to the global marketplace and to technological advances, corporations have had to streamline and downsize their management hierarchy. Organizations that used to pride themselves on offering lifetime employment and providing multilevel career ladders for the advancement of their managers have had to implement layoffs in order to stay competitive. As executives discovered that the middle manager's function of distributing information and tracking productivity could be accomplished more efficiently by computers, great numbers of middle management positions have been eliminated. The many layers of management, which formerly seemed essential, are now criticized as retarding responsiveness and inhibiting innovation.

The hierarchical, authoritarian structure of large organizations, which was based on restricted access to information, is giving way to self-managed work teams and the free flow of information in a flat, decentralized structure. Work teams are multifunctional and fluid, bringing together different kinds of workers whose expertise is needed for the current project.

One consequence of this structural change is that increasing numbers of workers are being hired on a project basis. Currently, more than one-third of the workforce, nearly 45 million Americans, are either self-employed or working as temporary employees, contract workers, part-timers, or consultants.

This fundamental restructuring of the nature of careers is most evident in large corporations, but there are competitive pressures on many organizations—large and small, for-profit and not-for-profit, private and public—to restructure and downsize their staff. Even in the professions of medicine and law, long-term employment is becoming less certain.

The implications of these ongoing changes for how you plan and develop your career are profound. Where once you could expect that being conscientious and capable would lead to lifetime employment, steady advancement, and salary increases, you now must prepare for an environment in which changing employers and even changing your career is the norm.

THE CHANGING NATURE OF WORK

The nature of work is also changing rapidly. Global competition and technological advances are changing what work needs to be done, by whom it is carried out, and how the work can be accomplished. Not only are job descriptions changing, but the future existence of many types of jobs is uncertain.

Structural changes in large organizations are changing the nature of work. With the sharp decrease in middle management positions and the corresponding increase in jobs on work teams, there is a new emphasis on teamwork skills. Being an effective team worker requires collaboration, communication, negotiation, and flexibility. Whereas middle managers usually make decisions individually, based on their authority in the hierarchy, most teams make decisions by consensus. Qualifying to be a member of a work team also requires having expertise that is needed by the team. When bringing together a project team, executives look for individuals with relevant skills and experience and a reputation for being effective and productive.

The increase in contingent workers in the workplace means adjustments for both employers and workers. The advantage to the employer of using contingent workers is the flexibility and cost-effectiveness of being able to adjust the workforce to meet the changing demands of the marketplace. The advantage to the worker is the release from full-time, lock-step employment and the opportunity to choose when, where, and for whom to work. However, the disadvantages for both the employer and the worker are substantial, including the lack of continuity and the threat of shortages—either of workers or of work. In addition, most nonpermanent employees receive no benefits—a substantial savings for the employer and a serious financial disadvantage for the employee.

Loyalty to an employer in the new workplace is augmented by loyalty to a profession or trade and its standards and ethics. The individual is motivated to give his best effort to accomplishing the mission of his employer because that is how he builds his professional reputation.

Another change is the strengthening of the diversity of the workforce as increasing numbers of women and minorities seek employment. It is predicted that white males will constitute only 15 percent of the 25 million new entrants that join the workforce by the year 2000. The remaining 85 percent will be white females, immigrants, and minorities of African-American, Hispanic, and Asian American origins (Hudson Institute, Inc., *Workforce 2000*). To achieve maximum advantage from incorporating men and women of diverse backgrounds and origins into work teams requires an appreciation of individuality and openness to differences.

REVISING YOUR EDUCATIONAL OBJECTIVES

How do you prepare for this changing world? It seems certain that college graduates who have developed their intellectual talents, analytical abilities, and communication skills will continue to be in demand. In addition, qualities such as flexibility, self-reliance, curiosity, and initiative will be highly valued. In planning your education, you should seek to develop expertise in the following areas to enhance your readiness to cope with the new workplace:

1. Learning skills—preparing for lifelong learning;
2. Experience with change—developing resilience and adaptability through meeting new challenges;
3. International experience—working or studying in a foreign country or countries and developing proficiency in a second language;
4. Use of computer technology—identifying and using computer applications;
5. Comfort with diversity—living and studying in a community of individuals of diverse backgrounds and ethnic and racial origins;
6. Teamwork experience—working in teams on both academic projects and extracurricular activities;
7. Work exploration—experiencing a variety of work environments through internships and short-term jobs;
8. Personal responsibility—taking charge of your educational planning and making the decisions that shape your own education.

Learning skills. College is a time of acquiring knowledge, but more importantly, it is a time of developing learning skills. Guided practice in researching questions, analyzing issues, synthesizing concepts, and solving problems prepares you for the necessity of continually increasing and diversifying your skills and expertise.

Experience with change. The ability to deal effectively with change increases with experience. It is important to select courses that will be intellectual adventures and to risk new experiences through college activities or jobs and internships. Experiences that challenge you to adapt your behavior will help you to develop resiliency and perhaps even to view change with enthusiasm.

International experience. The experience of living in a foreign country and the ability to communicate in a second language are already highly valued by many employers. By spending time working or studying in another country, you become more adaptable and self-reliant and gain knowledge of other cultures—all of which makes you better prepared for participation in the global economy.

Use of computer technology. "Comfort" with computers used to be sufficient, but now employers of liberal arts graduates expect them to have achieved "competence." This does not mean the ability to create software programs, but it does mean experience and confidence in using computers as tools for accomplishing work.

Comfort with diversity. Living and studying in a university community with individuals from diverse backgrounds helps you prepare for working with colleagues who are different from yourself. It provides you with the opportunity to appreciate the richness that can result when men and women of different racial and cultural backgrounds work together.

Teamwork experience. While individual achievement has traditionally been valued as fundamental in educational programs, more and more of society's work is accomplished by teams. Even in the university, interdisciplinary research teams have found that by working together they can achieve results that none of the team members could accomplish alone. To learn to work, communicate, and negotiate as a team member, it is important to include the experience of working in teams and of being evaluated as a team as part of your education.

Work exploration. To develop your skills and gain knowledge of work environments, you should take on a variety of responsibilities in your extracurricular activities, internships, and part-time and summer jobs. Writing for a campus publication, managing the tour of a chorale group, organizing a political action campaign, and tutoring children in an urban school are examples of opportunities to try out career-related tasks. In a similar way, summer jobs and internships give you a chance to engage in career-related work and to observe the work of established professionals.

Personal responsibility. To prepare for managing your own career, it is important that you take responsibility for planning your own education. The process of making decisions that shape your education, and living with the results of those decisions, prepares you for taking charge of planning your desired career expertise and selecting jobs which develop that expertise.

Opportunities to grow and develop in these areas are readily available during your undergraduate years. If you have completed your college education, you will have to seek out other ways to develop these attributes.

MYTHS THAT LINGER ON

If you take a job with a "good" organization, your employer will take care of your career development. Because of the impact of global competition and the evolving capabilities of new technologies, employers are no longer able to predict their personnel needs or even the management structure of their organizations over time. Therefore, they cannot offer lifetime employment to their employees.

Who you work for is more important than what work you do. The prestige of your employers used to be of primary importance, but now that new technology and global competition require leaders to continually reinvent their organizations, employers look for specific skills and accomplishments when evaluating job applicants. The position that offers you the opportunity to develop new skills and accomplish something is more important than the reputation of the employer.

The industry, organization, and position that you choose for your first full-time job determines the future course of your career. Not any longer. It is predicted that young persons now beginning their careers will have 8-10 different jobs during their work life and 2-3 different careers. As organizations restructure and jobs get redefined, individuals need to continually expand their skills and competencies.

BECOMING A CAREER ENTREPRENEUR

Because employers can no longer promise long-term employment, individuals must manage the development of their careers. In fact, the changing workplace offers individuals the opportunity to be "entrepreneurial" in the development of their careers.

What does it mean to be a career entrepreneur? Since it is not possible to know for certain what jobs and titles will exist in the future, you have to think in terms of trends, markets, and niches. Like the person who develops his own business, the career entrepreneur has to try to predict what the opportunities will be in the future. What skills will be in demand? What knowledge will be valued? What types of problem-solving abilities will be useful?

The goal of career planning can no longer be to target specific jobs. Deciding that you want to be vice president in five years does not make sense when the position of vice president in your organization may no longer exist by that time. Rather than setting your goal on a specific position ten years hence, you need to define what kinds of expertise you would like to have at that point.

Career planning today is like planning your college education. Goals should be defined in terms of skills, knowledge, and a record of accomplishments. Work opportunities should be evaluated in terms of the potential for increasing your expertise and expanding your experience. Which company you are working for will be less important than what you are learning and accomplishing. In fact, working as a temp might offer a better opportunity to develop skills and demonstrate competence than taking an entry-level job in a large corporation. Taking an assignment as a contract worker to accomplish a defined project might be the best way to expand your knowledge and reputation.

Because everyone's career "curriculum" will be unique, there will be no degrees or credentials to certify competence. Your growing expertise, documented record of accomplishments, and references from people with whom you have worked will be the foundation of your professional reputation and will enable you to move from one job to the next.

Whenever you are not learning on your job, it is time to consider making a change. To continue your learning curve, you might enlarge your responsibilities in your current job, move to a new job with the same employer, or change employers. In moving from job to job or employer to employer, you will probably want to plan a balance between staying with the same type of work and specializing in order to increase your skills and expertise, and making lateral moves that require learning new skills and adapting to a different work environment. Experience in a variety of environments which challenge you to transfer your skills and learn new skills and knowledge is a hedge against becoming redundant and may increase your employability. It will also increase your ability to deal with change.

Employment security rests on your employability, i.e., your reputation as a talented and productive worker. Employability is based on having skills and work experience that are in demand and a record of getting work accomplished.

As the business entrepreneur has to search continually for new markets for his product or service, the career entrepreneur has to look for new opportunities to expand his skills and knowledge. Those who are working on contract or as temporary employees know that their employment will end and that they will have to find new work. However, because it is predicted that one in three professionals will become the target of a layoff in his lifetime, every individual needs to have a plan for his next move.

An invaluable resource for you as a career entrepreneur is the development of a network of persons with whom you communicate about career issues. These will be people with whom you have a mutual interest in exchanging information and ideas about careers and work. Optimally, the people in your network will represent a variety of industries and professions. Some will be more advanced in their careers than you are, some will be just starting. In sharing career experiences with each other, you will each be gaining information that is potentially useful in planning your career development.

Having a network is of crucial importance for the career entrepreneur when moving from one job to the next. Studies show that most people find new jobs not by sending out resumes or responding to want ads, but by using connections. When an employer needs a job done, he is more comfortable hiring someone whom he knows or for whom he receives a personal recommendation from a colleague or friend. Members of your network can make your skills and accomplishments known to employers who have work that needs to be done.

There is also opportunity today for you to be entrepreneurial in designing your jobs. For example, increasing numbers of workers are becoming telecommuters, arranging to work from home or an office near home. Using the computer and communicating with colleagues and supervisors by electronic mail and fax, you might be able to work productively at home and save the time and hassle of commuting. Companies experimenting with telecommuting report a 25-35 percent increase in productivity.

Or, you may choose to work on contract so that you can exercise some choice over when, where, and for whom you work. Increasing numbers of workers are employed on a project basis as temps, part-timers, or consultants. This requires marketing yourself and your services and risking not being employed as much as you would like to be, but it does allow freedom of choice.

We are living in an era in which individuals can invent their own careers. Utilizing the information resources of the business entrepreneur, you can research trends and markets to identify skills and expertise for which demand is increasing. Choosing from these areas of expertise, you can target those skills that interest you and design a plan of jobs or contract work which provides the opportunity to learn those skills. As your expertise increases, you can seek out new markets and move on to new challenges.

Learning to Be Entrepreneurial

Being entrepreneurial is a state of mind which is characterized by looking for possibilities. An entrepreneurial person sees new opportunities in situations and events where others see only the status quo.

Being entrepreneurial is an approach to work which is creative and innovative. An entrepreneurial person thinks about and experiments with new ways to accomplish tasks, rather than accepting "the way we have always done it."

Being entrepreneurial is taking charge so that work gets accomplished. An entrepreneurial person takes the initiative to make something happen. He organizes, promotes, and manages the production of a new product or service.

Being entrepreneurial in one's career development involves all these abilities—seeing opportunities where others don't; seeking innovative ways to accomplish tasks; and persisting until progress is achieved.

What are the special skills of the career entrepreneur? The following stand out:

1. The ability to see opportunity where others see insurmountable hurdles
2. The ability to anticipate change as a challenge and an opportunity, the ability to be adaptable, flexible, and resilient, the ability to tolerate ambiguity and uncertainty

3. The ability to be innovative in marshalling resources to turn potential into opportunity
4. The ability to be disciplined and persistent in the pursuit of goals
5. The ability to learn from failure
6. The ability to assess one's strengths and weaknesses and to set goals for one's skill development

The chapters that follow describe the process and skills of exploring careers, making decisions about career direction, and conducting a search for work opportunities. The career entrepreneur must be proficient in all these areas, but he must also remain receptive to new possibilities which may present themselves at any time and from any source.

SOURCES

Job Shift: How to Prosper in a Workplace without Jobs. William Bridges. Addison-Wesley Publishing Co., Reading, MA, 1994.
Describes new ways of working and career development in a society without "jobs" as such. Bibliography. Indexed.

We Are All Self-Employed: The New Social Contract for Working in a Changed World. Cliff Hakim. Berrett-Koehler Publishers, San Francisco, CA, 1994.
Discusses the nature of career development in a work environment without traditional career ladders. Indexed.

Workforce 2000: Work and Workers for the 21st Century. Hudson Institute, Inc., Indianapolis, IN, 1987.
Examines trends in the U.S. economy and projects the demographic composition of the U.S. labor force by the year 2000. The research was funded by a grant from the Employment and Training Administration of the U.S. Department of Labor.

Chapter 2

CAREER EXPLORATION

INTRODUCTION

Developing Your Career, a Lifelong Process

Career development is a process that involves evaluating your present activities, assessing your skills and knowledge, clarifying long-term goals, and defining objectives for your next endeavor. Developing your career in the changing workplace requires that you engage in evaluation and planning throughout your lifetime.

We used to assume that careers would be made up of a series of positions with increasing status and income, often with one employer, but that is becoming rare as corporations restructure and streamline. As work shifts to project teams, many careers will be a history of projects accomplished, rather than positions held. The projects may vary in size and importance, and so may the financial compensation. There may be periods of unemployment between projects. As the person in charge of your career, you need to be continually on the lookout for work opportunities that move you toward your goals.

How career goals are defined is also changing. With the streamlining of management structures, it does not make sense to define your career goals in terms of positions. To decide that you want to be district manager in five years is unrealistic when the position of district manager might disappear in the interim. You need to define your career goals in terms of skills and expertise that you want to acquire and contributions that you want to make. Planning your career goals is like planning your education, setting objectives for the development of your talents, acquisition of knowledge, and accomplishments.

As discussed in Chapter 1, you will probably have many jobs and perhaps several careers in your lifetime. While some of the changes that you make will be of your own volition, others may be as the result of a layoff or of a project coming to an end. In recent years, many professionals and managers have found themselves unemployed unexpectedly because their services were no longer needed. The best way to prepare for unanticipated changes is to make planned changes on your own. If you have sought out opportunities to expand your skills and knowledge by taking on new challenges, a forced job change is not as paralyzing as if you had stayed in the same job with the same employer.

Developing your career requires exploring the world of work and yourself as a worker. Seeking to discover what kinds of work you find rewarding and satisfying is an investment in your future. Because we live in a time of rapid evolutionary change, your career exploration will continue throughout your lifetime. Whether you are in college or have been working for many years, now is the time to start.

Exploring Careers

Everything that you read, watch on television, and hear from other people can help you develop your career direction. As a career entrepreneur, you need to gather information from many sources to stay abreast of social, political and technological trends that might impact on your chosen line of work. Where will there be new opportunities and where will there be shrinking demands? What types of skills and expertise will be valued in the future?

As you explore the world of work, think about how society's needs are being met. Speculate on how these needs could be met more effectively. Think about how work is being accomplished now and how that might change in the future. In planning your career direction, think about where you want to make your contribution. What will be your mission? What would you like to accomplish? How do you want to invest your talents?

Your opportunities for exploring the world of work will vary depending on whether you are a college student or graduate student, or have a full-time job.

If you are a freshman, you have four years ahead of you to learn about the world around you and to think about what kind of contribution you want to make. You can plan a variety of experiences to gather information that will help you formulate both short-term and long-term goals. Each year you can add to your knowledge about the world of work and about yourself through extracurricular activities, term-time internships, part-time work, volunteer activities, summer jobs, or perhaps employment during a leave of absence. By arranging different summer jobs and by working and studying abroad, you can develop competence in dealing with change. If you are a freshman considering one of the few career fields with undergraduate course requirements, you may want to arrange activities and experiences which will help you evaluate that career field early in your college years.

If you are a junior or senior and wish to make decisions about what employment or graduate study to pursue after graduation, you may want to collect information more intensively. In this case, you might plan to spend several hours a week reading, talking to career advisers, and becoming involved in career-related experiences which will help you plan your next step.

If you have already graduated from college, you will probably want to find a job to support yourself while you explore career opportunities. It may be advisable to take a part-time job or work through a temp agency so that you can reserve some time during regular working hours for gathering career information.

If you are a graduate student and want to learn about the variety of career opportunities for Ph.D.'s, you may design career exploration experiences that can be integrated into your graduate program. For example, if teaching is not an expected part of your program, you may want to apply to be an instructor to develop teaching skills. Or, if you have not had administrative or management experience, you may want to offer to take responsibility for planning your departmental colloquia or for administering some part of the academic or advising program. If you are curious about career opportunities outside the university, you may want to identify some Ph.D.'s whom you can visit at work for information interviews. You might also want to arrange an internship or short-term job outside the university. In addition, broadening your academic program, perhaps by taking some electives in a professional school, can be intellectually challenging and rewarding. You may even find that considering your long-range career interests in combination with your present academic interests helps you choose a thesis topic of more lasting intellectual and personal meaning.

Exploring careers is an ongoing process. While you are a student, the academic schedule allows you time to explore work functions and career environments through student activities, internships, part-time jobs, and summer jobs. The variety of your experiences enables you to build a broader foundation for the continuing evolution of your career goals.

Planning Your Education

Many undergraduates assume that they must select their career field before they can select a concentration. This is not true. You do not need to major in economics to get a job in business. Nor do you need to major in science to get into medical school or major in computer science to get a job in the computer science industry. Law schools accept candidates from all concentrations.

Your choice of major should be based on your intellectual interests. What are you excited about studying? What do you want to know more about? With which faculty members would you like to take further coursework?

The Ph.D. program requires years of intensive, highly focused study in a chosen field. However, during your program, you make decisions that determine the breadth of your knowledge and experience in your discipline. Generally, broadening your areas of expertise, as well as having a variety of work experiences that enhance your professional development, increases your career opportunities when you complete your degree.

Some specific courses which may be taken as electives by undergraduates or graduate students are particularly relevant for certain types of employment. For example, if you are interested in business, it is helpful to take introductory courses in economics, computer science, and accounting. If you are interested in being a helping professional or teacher, be sure you include some introductory psychology or education courses in your program. If you are considering an international career, learn one or more foreign languages, take electives in the economics and politics of the region of your interest, and plan to spend time living and working abroad.

Upperclassmen and graduate students may wish to take electives in the graduate professional schools in their areas of career interest. Well-chosen electives can give you an introduction to the basic concepts and skills of a career field.

Learning from Career-Related Experiences

When analyzing career-related experiences, you should think about what you are learning about yourself as well as what you are learning about specific fields. It is important to gather information about each field that interests you, but it is equally important to recognize your feelings and reactions to the work, the people doing the work, and the work environment.

The most important step in getting to know yourself is learning to trust your self-perception. You can start by observing your own behavior, taking note of your feelings, thinking about your everyday choices, and observing your reactions to new environments.

Your friends, family, and coworkers are valuable sources of information. Their perceptions of you provide important data for you to consider. Ask them what kind of work they think that you would enjoy and what kind of work they think you would be good at. Take their advice seriously, but remember that you are the best authority on you.

The best way to learn about yourself in relation to the world of work is through exposure to different work environments. As you plan your career exploration, seek experiences that will give you new information or reinforce old information about yourself. The following are some of the questions to ask yourself:

- To what kind of work do I want to commit my talents, time, and energy?
- What kind of work do I find challenging and rewarding?
- What special talents do I have?
- In what type of environment do I work best?
- What kinds of relationships with people do I value?
- Are the objectives or products of the organization more important to me than my specific role?
- Is the social contribution of the work important to me?
- What priority do I give status, power, and level of income?
- How do my personal, educational, marriage, or family plans influence my career plans?

The best ways of gathering information about career fields include:

- Reading biographical, occupational, and professional literature;

- Interviewing and spending time with people in their places of employment;
- Working as a volunteer or for pay in the work environment so that you can observe what the professionals do and find out how they feel about their work.

What you want to learn about the career fields you are exploring depends on what is important to you. The next section, Work Dimensions, outlines some of the many aspects which you may want to think about when planning your career direction.

WORK DIMENSIONS

As you explore career fields, consider what is most important to you about the kind of work you want to do. The following discussion of work dimensions is presented to help you think about some of the characteristics of work and the environment in which it takes place. This outline is not meant to be comprehensive, but is intended to stimulate you to devise your own list of work dimensions.

Rewards System

Are the results of the work of the organization important to you? Is believing in the importance of your product or service more important to you than the specific tasks you are required to do?

Is the social value of the outcome of your labors important to you? What priority do you give the social value of your work in relation to other rewards, such as income, functions that you find challenging, or living in a particular geographic location?

Is public recognition or social status important to you? If you perform well in this career field, will people in the community know about your achievements? Will you be respected and admired for them?

Is the income potential in this career field satisfactory to you? What level of income would you expect in a starting position? What level would you expect in five years, ten years?

Do you think the daily functions of this work will be satisfying to you? Would you enjoy the doctor-patient relationship, the teacher-student relationship, the lawyer-client relationship? Would you feel rewarded by solving an important business problem, by designing a plan for marketing a new product, by assisting a new employee, or by becoming the leader of a team?

Is there opportunity to create or to accomplish something? Do you have a chance to analyze problems and to design solutions? Is there opportunity to bring something to completion? Do you have the chance to develop your own business?

Is there opportunity to increase your skills and expertise? Would this work challenge you to develop new competencies? Would you feel rewarded because you are continually learning?

Tasks and Functions

What kinds of problem solving does the work require? Does the work primarily involve organizing and processing data, building and operating equipment, or discovering, analyzing, and writing about ideas? Is a major portion of time spent in analysis and checking accuracy of details, or in the synthesis and development of ideas and plans?

What kinds of decision making does the job require? Is it possible to know all the pertinent facts before having to make a decision? Is it necessary to make decisions based on very little information? Does the job require taking risks and dealing with uncertainty?

Does the job require management of people? Is motivating and supervising people the main thrust of the job? Is negotiation a regular part of the work day?

Does the job involve working with people in helping relationships or persuasive relationships? Is the worker seen primarily as a person who helps others? Is the worker seen primarily as a person who sells products, services, or ideas?

Does the worker complete his work on his own, or does he work in collaborative team relationships? Does the worker have the opportunity to be recognized for personal accomplishment? Does the work involve teamwork and interdependent relationships? Does it involve negotiating and building consensus?

Is the problem solving or policy development focused on the local community, the larger U.S. community, another country or region, the global community? Will the results of the work impact on the welfare of a few people, many people, all people?

Styles

How is the job described? Do you know not only what you are supposed to do, but how you are supposed to do it? Is the job loosely described, stating only objectives, so that you may design the process of achieving the objectives? Are you given autonomy in how you achieve objectives?

Is it possible to do this work on a self-employed basis? Would working for yourself, on your own time, be suitable for you?

What is the pace of the work? Can you plan your work week in advance or is it unevenly paced, with unexpected new assignments with urgent deadlines, and slow times when there is little to do?

What are the hours that you are expected to work? Do most people in this field work from nine to five, or eight to six, or seven to seven? Do the people in this career work five or six or seven days a week? Do the hours tend to be irregular, with long hours at certain times of year?

How much variety is there in the work? Are the tasks and responsibilities different from one day to the next, from one hour to the next? Are there new types of problems to be solved? Is it the kind of job that, once you have a basic amount of experience, you can approach each day with confidence, feeling comfortable that you can accomplish what is expected of you?

Environment

Physical and Geographical Environment

What is the personal work space like? If the work takes place primarily at a desk, will that desk be in a large and spacious office which seems to communicate status and success, or will your office be one of a row of cubicles? Will your personal work space be an unimportant factor because you spend most of your day in other places? If your work requires being on the road, will your car serve as your office as you travel from client to client?

Could at least some of the work be done at home? Would it be possible to telecommute, working at home most days, but going into the office periodically?

Is the job likely to be in a rural setting or in a large city? Will your working day be spent indoors or outdoors, or some combination of both?

Will the work permit you to continue living in one place? Or will you be required, expected, or allowed to move from city to city, from country to country?

Does the job require travel? Will you have frequent business trips to interesting places? Will you spend most of your time away from your home base or most of your time in your home office? Will you have extended trips or international trips?

Will the work require that you live overseas for short periods of time, for several years, or for most of your career?

Organizational Environment

Does the organization have a nondiscrimination policy? Does management ensure that all candidates are considered for all positions on the basis of their qualifications and abilities without regard to race, color, sex, religion, age, national origin, citizenship, sexual orientation, or disability?

Is the organization committed to valuing diversity? Does the organization espouse the belief that a mutually respectful workforce that acknowledges and affirms its diversity is not only more productive, but also attracts and retains the best employees?

Is the organization highly structured, with clear definition of authority lines? Are the job descriptions explicit and detailed? Are the expectations clear? Does the supervisor pay attention to the details and daily progress of your work?

Is the organization loosely structured? Are the responsibilities defined in terms of objectives rather than in terms of the details of how the objective should be reached? Is the worker given little instruction and supervision and expected to devise his own way of fulfilling his responsibilities?

Is there opportunity for advancement? Is it clear what the criteria are for earning promotions? Does this organization tend to promote inside candidates or hire from outside?

Is there opportunity to start your own business, if you can make a better product or provide a better service? Is there the possibility of becoming a subcontractor or franchiser?

Human Environment

Are the relationships with fellow workers best characterized as competitive, collaborative, or cooperative? Do employees work alone on their own projects and compete with one another, or do they collaborate toward common goals? Does the job require working in interdependent relationships with colleagues?

Are the coworkers people with whom I will feel comfortable? Is the work environment free of discrimination and harassment of any kind? How are conflicts dealt with?

What kind of contacts, if any, does the worker have with people outside the organization? If a job requires meeting people, is the purpose of the meeting to help the client with a personal problem, to help the client with a professional problem, to teach the person something, to negotiate a contract, or to sell the person a product or a service?

If the organization is a service organization, what kind of population does it serve? Does it serve old people, young people, rich people, poor people, sick people, people who have serious personal problems? Do you want to work with the population the agency serves?

Some of the characteristics in this outline may not seem important to you. There may be other characteristics not mentioned that you will discover are very important to you.

Design your own outline to represent your view of the important dimensions of careers. You can use your outline to identify the characteristics of the career fields you are exploring and to analyze what you have learned about your personal preferences and priorities. As you become more clear about your priorities, the task of planning your goals and choosing your next step becomes easier.

IDENTIFYING CAREERS TO EXPLORE

There may be a career field that you have been focused on for some time. If so, your first objective in career exploration is to learn more about that field and evaluate the opportunities that it offers you.

If you are undecided about your career direction, the process of arriving at a list of fields to explore is your first opportunity to practice career decision making. You can then match what you know about yourself from your past experiences with a list of fields that you might consider. Make a list of four or five for your initial exploration. Bear in mind that as you expand your experiential knowledge of career fields, you will at the same time be increasing your knowledge of yourself; and, therefore, your list of career alternatives will continually evolve.

You have many resources from which to generate a list of careers to explore. The following resources are some of the most helpful.

Generating a List

Daydreams. When you dream about the future, what kind of work do you see yourself doing? What kind of skills and expertise do you have? What kind of role do you have in your community? What kind of organization do you work for? When you were twelve years old and thought about being an adult, what kind of career did you envision? If you haven't taken time to dream about the future recently, set aside some time when you can be by yourself in a relaxed and comfortable place and try to visualize your life in ten years.

Recommendations of Friends. During your years as a student, you have been working and living with peers who know you well. Have you asked your friends and roommates what career they think you would enjoy? They may suggest a career that you have not considered.

Recommendations of Teachers and Parents. People who know you well and care about you may have ideas about what career fields you would enjoy. Although you may think that their perceptions of you are inaccurate, incomplete, or outdated, it may be worth testing out their recommendations with some research and career-related experiences.

Lists of Occupations. There are many reference books which describe jobs and careers. Scanning the job titles listed in these books and reading about those that spark your curiosity helps you to expand your career horizons. *The American Almanac of Jobs and Salaries* and the *Occupational Outlook Handbook* are good places to start, as are the Career Advisor Series and the VGM Careers for You Series. If you are considering a government job, take a look at *The Federal Career Directory.* Do you want to use your language skills? You'll want to read *Foreign Languages and Your Career.* If you are concerned about the environment, peruse *The New Complete Guide to Environmental Careers. Careers in International Affairs* describes interesting careers with an international focus.

Learning from Your Experiences

Learning to think analytically about past and current experiences is a primary skill for developing career direction. Your experiences are the richest and most reliable source of data about what type of work you enjoy, what you find rewarding, and what stimulates you to perform at peak level. The following exercises will help you learn from your past experiences.

Your Special Accomplishments

Make a list of eight to ten accomplishments of which you are proud. Do not limit your list to achievements recognized by others; include achievements which you feel were milestones in your own development or important contributions to those around you.

1. Focus on these accomplishments one at a time and answer the following questions in writing:

    - Why do you feel proud of this achievement?
    - What were the rewarding and frustrating aspects?
    - What talents and abilities did it require?
    - What expertise did you develop?

2. When you have completed your analysis of the first accomplishment, take a clean sheet of paper and answer the same questions about the next achievement. In order to give yourself time to recall each experience in turn, you may want to spread this exercise over several days.

3. When you have answered these questions about each accomplishment, ask yourself the following:

    - Do these achievements have any common themes such as similar challenges, rewards, or objectives?
    - Do they require similar skills?
    - Do these characteristics seem related to any particular career fields?

You and Your College or Community

Make a list of organizations of which you have been a member in recent years.

1. Describe in writing your participation in these activities, one at a time.

   • Why did you choose to participate in this activity?
   • Describe your relationship to the work of the group and to other members of the group.
   • List the positions of responsibility to which you were elected, were appointed, and volunteered for in each group.
   • What did you enjoy most about this group?

2. When you have completed describing the first activity, take a clean sheet of paper and describe your work in the second activity.

3. When you have answered these questions about each group, look for common themes in your participation.

   • Were there similar reasons that you chose each activity?
   • Did you usually take a leadership role?
   • Were you more inclined to seek a role in which you could make a contribution, but not be responsible for the work of others?
   • Were you the person who initiated new activities, the person from whom others sought advice, or the person who made sure that everyone felt included?
   • How would you characterize your role in each group?

Analyzing what you do in your volunteer activities can give you insight into your values as well as into what types of relationships and functions you prefer in organized activity.

These exercises will get you started in this important process of learning about yourself by analyzing your experiences. Engaging in this process enables you to identify the characteristics of work that are important to you. Chapter 3 will discuss career decision making in greater detail and will list some sources that can guide you through this process.

Taking Vocational Interest Inventories

Vocational interest inventories can provide information that gives you new insights and assists you in evaluating what you have learned from experience. An inventory asks you questions about your preferences, and from your answers, generates a profile of your interests. Your interest profile is then correlated with the profiles of people in different occupations. These correlations can help you select career fields to research. It is important to remember that these tests will not tell you about your abilities, only about your interests and values.

Meeting with a counselor to discuss your interest test results will help you understand them. You may want to develop a plan for exploring the careers with which you have a similar interest pattern. In addition, thinking creatively about this profile of occupations can help you identify work characteristics that are important to you and that you want to keep in mind as you evaluate career opportunities.

Working with a Career Counselor

By listening to the thoughts and feelings that you express about yourself, your past experiences, and your future, a career counselor may be able to help you gain new and clearer insight into what you have to offer and what you are looking for in your career. Your career counselor can help you translate what you have learned from your past experiences into career-related skills and characteristics. If you have already identified several careers which you wish to explore, your counselor will help you to outline a plan for experiential research. If you do not yet have a list of careers to explore, that will be your first objective.

What is the best way to find a career counselor? Your college or university career office should be your first stop. Many institutions offer counseling not only for currently enrolled students, but also for alumni. If your college does not have such services available to you, they might be able to recommend a career counseling service for you.

Another source is your local public library. A reference librarian should be able to help you to identify local organizations that offer career guidance or can refer you to directories like the *Directory of Counseling Services* or the *National Directory of Certified Counselors*.

There are many career and vocational counselors in private practice.

Some advertise in local newspapers or can be found in the classifieds; others might be recommended to you by friends.

Evaluate a career counselor as you would any other professional from whom you seek services. Ask for credentials and references, as well as fees, and whether there is a sliding scale. State clearly your objectives and what kind of assistance you think you need. Recognize that personalities are a factor; you may not be comfortable with a specific personality or approach to career planning. After all, you are a unique person with your own needs and objectives.

Maintaining Your Career Research File

Careful records are essential to keeping track of your career research. Whether you use a card file, folders, notebooks, or a computer database, you must be able to retrieve information about people that you have contacted, employers to whom you have written, and jobs to which you have applied. Take care to record dates, names, titles, addresses, and telephone numbers accurately for future reference.

It is advisable to take notes on everything you read and make lists of people you would like to contact. Keep copies of all your correspondence and record dates and notes on all telephone calls. After each interview, make notes of information you learned, the observations you made, and the impressions you formed. You may want to keep a journal about your experiences and reactions.

The next three sections discuss three different sources of information about careers: reading materials such as books, pamphlets, magazines, and newspapers; people in the careers that you are exploring; and short-term jobs or internships.

USING CAREER LITERATURE

What's Out There

This is a question that you should keep asking yourself throughout your lifetime. What's out there that I might be interested in? What's happening that might impact on my current work? Where might there be new opportunities for a person with my expertise?

Even when you are just beginning to learn how to research career fields, you will probably have some knowledge about possibilities that exist out there in the "real world." You may even be familiar with the specifics of a field or two. But what about the rest of the possibilities in the world of work? What about those areas of employment you've never heard of, or whose names conjure a fuzzy image in your mind? How do you go about getting more information about them? You do something you're probably very good at by now: you research!

No matter how busy you are with your current activities, arrange to spend some time reading about careers and people in different professions. This is an investment of time that will pay for itself many times over. You will learn about what people find interesting and rewarding in their chosen work. From reading the journals and magazines they read, you will learn about the problems and issues that concern professionals in different fields and will acquaint yourself with their vocabularies and styles of expression. More importantly, you will find yourself beginning to identify aspects of professions that you like or dislike.

Where Do You Start?

Try the annotated bibliographies at the end of each chapter in this book, but pay special attention to the one at the end of this chapter. The sources listed under the headings Career Descriptive Literature, Directories of Career Literature and Counselors, and Directories of Trade and Professional Journals and Associations will become valued companions in this search and your ongoing career exploration. The more you use these references, the more comfortable you will be with them, and the more information you will be able to extract from them.

The bibliographies provide you with examples of the kinds of information to look for and the likely sources for finding them. Scan the Index of Resources by Career Field in the Appendix. If you don't find the exact career field you're looking for, pick something that might be related. Then refer back to this chapter's bibliography to get a start: the *Occupational Outlook Handbook* and the *Subject Guide to Books in Print* should launch your search.

What Next?

Consult one of the periodical directories. *The Gale Directory of Publications and Broadcast Media,* although of particular interest to someone wishing to enter the magazine publishing field, will provide the names of trade and professional journals in a wide range of fields. This will enable you to begin reading what the professionals in your field of interest read. The journals may have interesting book reviews and may provide the names of people prominent in the field. Find out more about these individuals by checking biographical dictionaries and directories, which you can identify by using *Directories in Print* or the *Gale Directory of Databases.*

    Directories in Print will prove useful to you again later in your search when you want to identify potential employers in a particular field. For instance, here you will find a reference to the *Consultants and Consulting Organizations Directory* (listed in the bibliography at the end of Chapter 4), which will enable you to find out who does management, health care, or environmental consulting, or consulting in any number of other specialized areas. It will also help you to identify what the possibilities are in the world of consulting and to match those opportunities against your own subject strengths and interests.

Is This Really as Complicated and Confusing as It Sounds?

It doesn't have to be. The key to using career literature and other reference materials to your advantage is to maintain an open mind and to follow up on the interesting facts you discover. This is where your career research file proves its worth. If, for example, you jot down the name of the professional association that is mentioned in a newspaper article, later on you can consult the *Encyclopedia of Associations* to get an address or phone number and to see if the group publishes a newsletter or journal.

    You will develop certain habits almost subconsciously. By reading the *Wall Street Journal* or other trade or professional publications with pen and pad close by, you can jot down the names of interesting companies or organizations almost without thinking. While scanning articles for names of individuals prominent in a particular field, you can keep an open mind for new information, such as a job title you've never seen before. The quest for more information about this job in the

Occupational Outlook Handbook will lead you to related or similar positions.

Does It Ever End?

No. After you have secured your first position, you will continue to explore paths open to you. As you have new experiences and increase your areas of expertise, your career interests will continue to develop. As your life changes, so will your career priorities. You may find yourself moving from the private sector to the public or nonprofit sector, and then back again. Geographic location may become a factor if you are in a two-career relationship, causing you to limit your explorations to a certain part of the country or to relocate to another area. If so, directories with geographic indexes will facilitate your search.

As you refine your career research skills and allow your imagination to lead you, possibilities will continue to unfold. When you combine your book learning with visiting and interviewing career advisers, the differences in the dimensions of various career fields will become clearer to you.

INTERVIEWING CAREER ADVISERS

People are the best source of information about careers. Careers do not exist as objective phenomena which become superimposed on a person's life. The responsibilities and requirements of a particular position influence the daily life of the person, but each individual meets those demands differently and thereby develops a career experience which is unique. To get a personal view of how someone is developing his career and how he experiences it. you must interview him. Most people, even busy people, enjoy talking with a young person who has a sincere interest in learning about their careers.

It is preferable to visit people at work so that you may observe the activities, environment, and human community in which the work takes place. It is likely that the person you are interviewing will give more realistic information and impressions about his work if you meet with him at his workplace than if you meet in a social setting. After your visit, be sure that you write a thank-you note immediately. If you hope to meet with the person in the future, send a follow-up letter later, reporting on your progress.

Remember that every person you visit may be someone with whom you will want to stay in contact. Each of these conversations may be the beginning of a relationship that will be sustained over time by the sharing of information and mutual interests. This is how your network gets started: by identifying and staying in touch with people who share your professional interests.

Identifying Potential Advisers

The career offices of many colleges have files of the names of alumni who have volunteered to serve as career advisers. These women and men are valuable sources of information and advice about their profession or geographic location.

Career panels held by college career offices and by professional associations are an excellent way to meet people who might become career advisers for you. If you are particularly interested in a speaker on a career panel, introduce yourself to him after the meeting and ask if it would be possible to set up a time for an individual conference. If it is not possible to talk with the speaker at the meeting, find out his name and address from the host so that you can write to introduce yourself and to request an opportunity to meet.

There are many special visitors at a university each year. Some stay for only a few days, others stay for a full academic year. When you hear about a person coming as a lecturer or as a guest performer in the arts, contact the office hosting the visitor ahead of time to see if there will be an opportunity for you to have an individual conference with that person. Even if this introductory interview is brief, the visitor may agree to have you visit him at work to learn more about his career field.

Visiting Fellows are often interested in getting to know students. They usually accept with enthusiasm invitations to come to your dining hall for lunch or dinner. If you take the initiative to become acquainted with Visiting Fellows early in the year, you may find that by the end of the year you have made a friend — someone who is established in a field that interests you and can give you very pertinent career advice and assistance in your job hunt.

Another source of career advisers is friends of your parents, and the parents and friends of your roommates. You can arrange to meet these people when you are at home or when visiting a roommate during vacations. Even if this friend is the person who lives next door, it is preferable that your interview for career advice take place at his office rather than at home.

Local alumni groups are an excellent resource for career advisers. You can also identify potential career advisers from people mentioned in professional journals and magazines and authors of articles that interest you. There are directories listing people in almost every line of work: the title index in *Directories in Print* lists several columns of books beginning with *Who's Who in* . . . There are the industry directories, like *Editor and Publisher International Yearbook*, the *Thomson Bank Directory*, or the *National Directory of Children, Youth, & Families*, which give names of officers as well as names and addresses of organizations. Letters to these people stating that you are interested in their career field and asking if you may meet with them at their place of work are likely to receive positive responses. Be sure to make it clear that you are not asking for a job; you are seeking information and advice that will help you plan your career.

Preparing for the Initial Interview

It is important that you read the occupational literature and professional publications of the adviser's career field before you visit him. If the adviser works for a large corporation or organization, read the annual report of the organization. If the adviser works in the federal government in Washington, look up his name in *Carroll's Federal Directory* to find out his title and position, and research his agency in *The United States Government Manual*. If he is a member of Congress, you will find a list of his committee memberships in *The Almanac of American Politics*, the *Congressional Staff Directory*, or the *Congressional Yellow Book*. If you're planning to visit an adviser at an advertising agency, check the *Standard Directory of Advertising Agencies* to see what accounts his firm handles. *Literary Market Place* will tell you what kinds of books a publisher publishes. *Public Interest Profiles* describes the activities and political orientation of organizations involved in public policy matters, from environmental groups to think tanks. In short, show the adviser that you cared enough to do some research!

To make an appointment with a career adviser, you may call him on the telephone or send a letter and resume and follow up with a telephone call. Whichever way you arrange the appointment, it is advisable to take a resume with you to the interview. If you hand the adviser a resume at the beginning of the interview to introduce yourself, he does not need to ask you about your background and you may focus the conversation on learning about his work. For advice on making telephone calls, writing letters and resumes, and interviewing, see Chapter 6.

Planning What You Want to Learn from a Career Adviser

The most important outcome of an information interview is understanding another person's career experience. You want to learn what the career adviser finds rewarding in his work and what he finds frustrating. As he shares what he has experienced as the reality in his chosen field, you will be able to sense whether his enthusiasm about his work stems primarily from his daily tasks and responsibilities, from the people with whom he works, from his commitment to the objectives of his work, from financial or other rewards, or from all of these characteristics.

Before you meet with the adviser, it is important to develop questions that will elicit the information you want. The following list will give you a place to start:

- the satisfactions and rewards that he values
- the challenges of his daily work
- the skills and expertise that he is developing
- the problems he thinks about
- the types of decisions he makes
- the programs that he is creating/managing
- his long-range and short-range objectives
- his relationships with coworkers and clients
- the steps he took to arrive at his present position

It is interesting to seek his advice on the best way to enter the field, how to prepare for entry-level positions, what reading you should do to increase your understanding of the field, and what part-time or short-term work experiences will provide opportunities to evaluate your interest in his field. Before you leave, be sure to ask him if there are other people that he would suggest that you speak with. If you would like to spend a day or two shadowing or observing the career adviser, it is reasonable to ask, but be aware that the adviser may not be able to accommodate you.

If the interview has been informative and helpful, tell him so. Don't hesitate to express your interest and enthusiasm. Let the adviser know why this conversation has been valuable to you.

Observing the Work Environment and the People

An important aspect of your visit to a career adviser is the opportunity to observe and react to the environment in which the adviser works. Do you like the physical surroundings? Perhaps the adviser will take you on a tour of the office so that you are able to meet other people and observe what they are doing. This exposure gives you an opportunity to see how people interact in the environment and to learn how the functions and tasks are managed.

Take note of your reactions to every aspect of the situation. Do you find this an exciting place to be? Are the people interesting to you? Would you like to be doing what they are doing? Would you like your working life to be like theirs?

After each interview, make notes for your career research file on the information and advice you received, the observations you made of the work environment, and your reactions to the adviser and his work.

Saying Thank You

It is important to write a **thank-you letter** and send or deliver it within twenty-four hours after each interview. If some questions have occurred to you after the interview, feel free to ask them in this letter. If you plan to contact people whom he has recommended to you or to arrange experiences which he suggested, make sure you report your progress in a follow-up letter or telephone call. Remember that each career adviser is a valuable human resource to you. Having shared some of his personal career experiences, he will be very interested in hearing from you periodically about how your career is developing. If you keep in touch, the relationship may last many years.

Building Your Network

These relationships with people who share your professional interests are the foundation of your network. They can become your professional friends, and they may or may not be social friends as well. When you are young and new in the working world, most of the members of your network will be older and have more years of experience than you have. They can be helpful to you by sharing what they have learned from their experiences, advising you on your career strategy, and referring you to others who might be helpful to you. But how can you be helpful to them? As you meet with people in the industry that you are exploring, you pick up interesting information about what's going on. It can be very helpful to members of your network if you keep in touch and share information that you are gathering.

Of course, you can't keep in touch with everyone that you meet. You will make choices about how frequently you want to stay in touch with members of your network based on whether you have mutual interests and can be helpful to each other.

ARRANGING CAREER-RELATED EXPERIENCES

Spending time in the workplace and observing or assisting with the work of a professional gives you insight into the skills and expertise of the professional, a feeling for his work environment, and knowledge about yourself which you cannot learn from books.

Extracurricular Activities

In the college community, there are many opportunities to learn career-related skills and to test your career interests. You can explore whether you enjoy management responsibility by serving as the manager of a music organization or athletic team, or by producing a show. You can learn about advertising and marketing by being the business manager of a student publication or a manager of a campus business or service. You can experience the excitement and frustrations of journalism by writing for a student newspaper. You can learn about teaching, advising, and evaluating people by being a tutor or teaching fellow. You can be a counselor to your fellow students as a member of a peer counseling group. You can have the experience of helping people in need or working toward improving their welfare through peer counseling services or community service programs. You can participate in campus organizations related to politics and government, or you can become an active participant in student government and student/faculty advisory groups. Student organizations offer you the opportunity to develop career-related skills and to serve your college community at the same time.

Short-Term Jobs/Internships

Outside the college community, there are many opportunities for you to have career-related work experiences. Summers, leaves of absence, and term-time employment provide opportunities to arrange short-term jobs or internships to learn about a variety of different work environments. If you do a different kind of work each summer, you will learn a great deal about yourself and about potential careers. It is important not to focus too early. Regard these opportunities for short-term work experience as "career electives" and try to experiment as broadly as possible. If you can, try to plan at least one summer abroad.

Although you will not ordinarily have the same responsibilities in these work experiences as you would have in a full-time position, you will be able to experience the work environment. You have the chance to observe at close range the daily tasks and interactions of professionals working in the field. For example, an orderly in a hospital has the opportunity to observe doctors' interactions with patients and to see how the behavior of the doctor affects both the patients and the staff. At the same time, the orderly fulfills some important functions in the care of patients. The business intern will not usually be given management responsibilities, but will be assigned projects that relate to management functions. The intern will also have the opportunity to observe the managers' daily activities.

Some of your jobs during college will be "student" jobs which you take because you need to earn money. Although these jobs may not be in a work environment that you would consider after you graduate, every job provides the opportunity to learn general skills, such as getting along with your supervisor and fellow workers, adapting to the culture of the workplace, and fulfilling your responsibilities. These general work skills will be important to later employers.

Career Exploration Opportunities with Varying Time Commitments

There are a variety of career exploration activities which require different levels of commitment and different allotments of time. You may start at any time that suits your schedule and needs. Each type of activity offers you direct personal experience in a vocational field of your choice.

Career Forums. Career fairs or forums where a large number of employers are present to talk to people about their company and career field are an opportunity to gather information about working in a variety of careers in a short period of time.

Career Advisers. As little as thirty minutes with a career adviser can provide you with a wealth of information not generally available through other sources. To prepare for the visit, read about the adviser's career field and organization so that you have some basic understanding of his work. Plan to arrive early so that you have time to observe the work environment and perhaps chat with the receptionist. When you meet the adviser, shake his hand and make eye contact. To tell him a little about yourself, hand him a copy of your resume. After the exchange of initial pleasantries, you can then lead off the conversation by inquiring about what he finds rewarding in his work. This focuses the interview on rewards and satisfactions and is more likely to generate a more interesting conversation.

Shared Experience. By talking to career advisers or your career counselor, you may be able to identify a professional in your field of interest whom you could visit for several hours or for a day or two. During such a visit, you could observe the daily activities of that professional and his colleagues. In a profession such as architecture or consulting, you might be able to get hands-on experience assisting on a specific project.

Short-Term Internships/Experiences. Some colleges or alumni clubs offer internship programs during college vacations which provide the opportunity for you to spend one to five days visiting a professional at work. You can sometimes arrange your own brief internships by expressing interest in spending a day or several days with a career adviser to learn the variety of activities, decisions, and interactions he engages in on a typical day.

Term-time Internships/Jobs. If you are ready to commit ten to twenty hours a week to career exploration, you can apply for internships. Interns usually have some specific responsibilities which make them part of the work team, and often there is the opportunity to take on extra, more interesting responsibilities. Media and the arts are two fields in which experience as an intern is almost essential in order to be competitive for paid jobs. There are clearinghouses and directories for internships and volunteer opportunities in almost all fields. Some states and cities have offices that generate internship listings. In addition, the directories listed in the Internships and Summer Work section of the bibliography at the end of this chapter will help you to identify other resources.

Summer Jobs/Internships. College summers offer a special opportunity for short-term, full-time work experience in the U.S. or abroad. If you do not have to earn money, you can probably arrange almost any kind of experience anywhere in the world. If you need to earn money, as most students do, you should start in the fall term to search for a paid summer job or internship in the career field that you are exploring. If you are unable to find a paid opportunity, you could take an unpaid internship in order to gain experience and work a second job to earn money. Frequently, employers offering an unpaid summer internship will expect only about thirty hours a week because they assume that you will have some kind of part-time employment.

If you are interested in science, you may want to arrange to do research at least one summer. There are numerous possibilities in government and nonprofit research labs and in faculty members' labs. Paid summer internships in government labs are competitive and the application deadlines are early in the winter. There is usually opportunity to gain research experience in faculty members' labs, but paid positions are rare. Faculty members who have grant money to pay a research assistant during the summer usually select that student from among those who have been unpaid research assistants during the term. At some colleges, students can apply for a grant to support summer research experience.

Books like *Peterson's Internships* will introduce you to internships and summer jobs, as will the various volumes of the Career Advisor

Series. *The New Careers Directory: Internships and Professional Opportunities in Technology and Social Change* will lead you to summer opportunities in public and community service organizations. You can also identify potential employers in various industry or trade directories listed in the bibliography at the end of Chapter 4.

A summer job hunt should be conducted in the same way as any other job hunt. Chapter 6 contains advice on preparing your resume, writing cover letters, and interviewing with potential employers. Start early! Search broadly, and be sure to apply for a variety of opportunities.

Leave of Absence/Interim Employment. A leave of absence provides you with the opportunity to be a full-time worker in an organization and a self-supporting adult, perhaps in a new community or overseas. Because you commit yourself for a longer time, employers are usually willing to give you more responsibility.

You can start your job search by looking through internship directories to get ideas about opportunities that are available. You may apply for and get one of the internships listed. Or you might choose to arrange your own work opportunity, selecting a type of work you want to experience or a place where you want to live. If you are persistent in your search, you will surely be able to arrange an interesting learning experience.

For your first job after graduation, you will want to look for an opportunity that challenges you to learn and that requires that you develop skills. No matter what work you are doing, you want to be continually increasing your skills and expertise and your self-understanding.

ENRICHING YOUR EDUCATION
WITH INTERNATIONAL EXPERIENCE

The adventure of working or studying abroad adds a special dimension to your education and is valuable preparation for participating in the global economy. Living in a foreign culture, learning different ways to meet daily needs and build relationships, and trying to understand different perspectives on national and international issues expands your awareness of the diversity of human cultures. Being away from the country in which you grew up also provides the opportunity to see yourself more clearly and to think about how you might want to contribute during your lifetime. *The Harvard Guide to International Experience* is a good place to begin your research as you plan your overseas adventure.

If you spend time abroad, you will be challenged to be more independent than you have ever been before, a prospect that is as exciting as it is daunting. You will have the chance to prove to yourself that you can cope in new and different environments, that you can be flexible, adaptable, and self-reliant.

Depending on where you choose to go, you will experience varying degrees of cultural differences. If you go to a non-English-speaking country, you will have a chance to increase your language skills. You will discover that there are different ways of structuring work and the professions to meet human needs. You will learn different expectations and customs regarding marriage, family, and community. Living and working or studying in another country is exciting and mind-expanding. Far from the comforts of familiar surroundings, you become involved in a different culture, learning new ways and perspectives on life.

When Should I Go?

Your timing will be influenced by what you want to do and your **language preparation**, since you want to have some familiarity with the language of the country before you go. If you are an undergraduate, you may want to arrange an internship or job in a foreign country during the summer or a leave of absence or for the year after graduation. You could volunteer to work in a mission hospital, in an orphanage, on an environmental education project, or in a development agency. The books listed in the Work and Study Abroad section of the bibliography at the end of this chapter will give you many ideas of activities to consider.

Many kinds of work opportunities are possible, such as teaching English, serving as a research assistant, or writing for an English-language newspaper, but you do have to inform yourself about work permit regulations. Short-term work permits for some countries may be obtained while you are a student or even as a graduating senior, from the Council on International Educational Exchange.

If you decide to study at a foreign university, you can apply to one of the many programs sponsored by U.S. institutions or you can apply directly to the university as a special student, if your language preparation is adequate. At most colleges you can petition for degree credit for coursework done at another university, but you may have to be prepared to study in the local language. Because you will have to plan in advance when these activities will best fit into your academic program, it's never too early to start thinking about where you would like to go, and what you would like to study.

Another good time to arrange an experience abroad is after graduation. The internship or job you arrange might be directly or tangentially related to your career. It might be a time you set aside for a special experience in human service through the Peace Corps or some other international volunteer organization.

If you are a graduate student, you may be spending your time abroad doing thesis research and writing. There are predoctoral and postdoctoral fellowships and internships at foreign universities and in international organizations such as the United Nations. The funding references such as *Financial Aid for Research and Creative Activities Abroad* and *Financial Aid for Study and Training Abroad* listed in the Work and Study Abroad section of the bibliography at the end of this chapter will be of particular interest to you.

Deciding Where to Go

Read everything you can and talk to as many people as you can. Find out who among your friends has been abroad and meet with them to discuss their experiences. Ask your instructors and career counselor for suggestions. Contact alumni of your college who live abroad or the officers of alumni clubs in foreign countries. Do all the things you would do if you were trying to find out about opportunities in the U.S., but in addition, study the language of the country where you want to go.

Finally, be realistic. Choose an activity and location that will be enriching and challenging, but be aware of the adjustments you will have to make. Find out as much as you can about the work opportunity and its responsibilities, living arrangements, housing, diet, health and safety precautions, transportation, and isolation from other Americans. Unless you are proficient in the language, look for programs for language training and orientation to the culture.

EXPANDING YOUR HORIZONS BY EXPERIENCING THE UNFAMILIAR

Whether the adventures you plan during your career exploration take you into new worlds at home or abroad, you will expand your knowledge about careers by taking risks. It takes courage to walk into a new job, to move to a new city, to begin work in a new environment where you don't know anybody. It can be a little scary, but the potential for learning about yourself and new career options is worth some risk.

Taking on new responsibilities in unfamiliar surroundings is a way of testing yourself. New challenges allow you to discover talents and abilities that you did not know you had. Having to relate to different people in a new organization develops your understanding of individual differences. Experiencing new worlds of work expands your knowledge of the diversity of career opportunities.

Getting away from the familiar and comfortable is a way of getting to know yourself. Meeting the challenge of becoming productive in a new environment helps you identify new strengths and increases your self-confidence. Being separated from the people most significant to you provides the opportunity to see more clearly who you are, apart from and because of these relationships. Distance makes it possible to view the possibilities in your familiar surroundings more objectively.

Moving to a job in an unfamiliar environment requires that you develop the ability to deal with change. Learning to apply your skills to new tasks and to work effectively in a different culture will prepare you for future changes in your work. Because we live in a time of accelerating change, **employers look for individuals who are not only experienced in dealing with change, but who see it as a positive challenge.**

The risks involved in adventures into new worlds can be minimized by careful research and preparation. From reading and talking to knowledgeable people, you can become informed about customs, mores, and expectations. If you have the opportunity to talk in advance with people in the new organization, you can glean information and advice that will help you to get a good start.

Unless you experiment in new worlds, you are not really exploring! Don't cheat yourself of the excitement of new adventures. There are many resources that you can use to plan horizon-expanding adventures in this country and abroad. Those listed in the bibliography at the end of this chapter will give you a good start, as will the job-hunting resources at the end of Chapter 4. All you have to do is take the first step!

SOURCES

Career Descriptive Literature

The American Almanac of Jobs and Salaries, 1994-1995 ed. John W. Wright. Avon Books, New York, NY, 1993.

> Examines various positions in the public, private, and nonprofit sectors, with much of the salary information taken from Department of Labor and Department of Commerce data. Includes information on special groups, like temporary workers, women, minorities, new college graduates, etc. Indexed.

America's Top Medical and Human Service Jobs, 2nd ed. J. Michael Farr. JIST Works, Inc., Indianapolis, IN, 1994.

> Provides an overview of market trends, as well as descriptions of jobs, including skills and training required. Contains a separate chapter on career planning and job-search strategies.

Career Advisor Series. Bradley J. Morgan and Joseph M. Palmisano, editors. Visible Ink Press, Detroit, MI, 1992-1994.

> Career guides for twenty different fields, each of which is packed with information about the field and ideas for getting started, including lists of potential employers, internships, and sources of further information.

Careers in International Affairs. Maria Pinto Carland and Daniel H. Spatz, Jr., editors. School of Foreign Service, Georgetown University, Washington, DC, 1991.

> An introduction to international work in a variety of settings, including business, education, government, media, nonprofits, research, and international organizations. Identifies and describes potential employers and provides addresses. Bibliography. Organization index.

Careers in International Law. Mark W. Janis, editor. Section of International Law and Practice, American Bar Association, Washington, DC, 1993.

> Describes careers in both the private and public sectors. Appendixes list addresses of international organizations and nongovernmental organizations dealing with international issues in Washington, DC, as well as ABA-approved foreign summer programs.

Choosing a Career in the Law. Dena O. Rakoff. Office of Career Services, Faculty of Arts and Sciences, Harvard University, Cambridge, MA, 1991.

> Gives an overview of the profession, describes the law school application process and curriculum, and introduces some law-related fields. Lists additional sources of information.

Dictionary of Occupational Titles, 4th ed., revised 1991. U.S. Department of

Labor, Employment and Training Administration. The Career Press Inc., Hawthorne, NJ, 1992.

Contains approximately 17,500 job titles and their definitions, arranged by type of occupation. A good way to get an overview of the different job possibilities within a given field, although not all will be of interest to the liberal arts graduate. Occupational title and industry indexes.

Federal Career Directory. United States Office of Personnel Management. Superintendent of Documents, U.S. Government Printing Office, Washington, DC, 1990.

Describes federal career and employment opportunities, including internship and student employment programs.

Foreign Languages and Your Career, 4th ed. Edward Bourgoin. J. Audio-Forum, Guilford, CT, 1993.

Introduces the various career fields in which foreign language skills are important or necessary. Lists additional sources of information, including organizations. Index of occupations.

Guide to Careers in World Affairs, 3rd ed. Foreign Policy Association. Impact Publications, Manassas Park, VA, 1993.

Describes opportunities in the international job market in both the U.S. and abroad. Includes internship and application information. Chapters on graduate programs and job-hunting strategies. Annotated bibliography. Indexed.

Guide to Cruise Ship Jobs, revised ed. George Reilly. Pilot Books, Babylon, NY, 1994.

Describes the jobs available and gives job-hunting tips. Lists major cruise lines and firms that recruit for cruise ship companies. Basic nautical glossary.

The Harvard College Guide to Careers in Government and Politics. Lynn Bracken Wehnes. Office of Career Services, Faculty of Arts and Sciences, Harvard University, Cambridge, MA, 1992.

A beginner's manual for those contemplating employment in government and politics, with references to additional sources of information for the job seeker. Chapters on Capitol Hill jobs, campaign work and political consulting, and opportunities in the executive branch, international organizations, state and local government, think tanks, etc.

The Harvard College Guide to Consulting, 2nd ed. Marc P. Cosentino. Office of Career Services, Faculty of Arts and Sciences, Harvard University, Cambridge, MA, 1993.

Introductory information on consulting in general, followed by essays on the specialties within the field, each written by an expert practitioner. Includes sample interview questions and case interviews. Appendixes contain firm profiles and address list. Glossary.

The Harvard College Guide to Investment Banking. Marc Cosentino. Office of Career Services, Faculty of Arts and Sciences, Harvard University, Cambridge, MA, 1990.

> Chapters on corporate finance, public finance, sales and trading, entry-level positions, and retail brokerage. Includes four appendixes: dilemmas and decisions, internships, sample resumes, and a reading list. Glossary.

The Harvard Guide to Careers in Mass Media. John H. Noble. Office of Career Services, Faculty of Arts and Sciences, Harvard University, Cambridge, MA, distributed by Bob Adams, Inc., Holbrook, MA, 1989.

> Profiles eight career fields within the entertainment media, news media, publishing, and promotional media. Includes annotated bibliographic references, case studies, and job-hunting tips.

Jobs in Arts and Media Management. Stephen Langley and James Abruzzo. ACA Books, New York, NY, 1992.

> Describes the various career fields and offers job-hunting advice. Lists graduate programs in arts administration, arts and media management internships, seminars, workshops, information centers, referral services, membership associations, and periodicals with job listings.

Jobs '95. Kathryn and Ross Petras. Simon & Schuster, New York, NY, annual. (Title changes with year.)

> Contains career outlooks by field, industry forecasts, and a regional profile of employment prospects. Lists additional sources of information, as well as major employers by industry and state. .

Market Wizards: Interviews with Top Traders. Jack D. Schwager. Harper Business, New York, NY, 1993.

> Includes traders from a variety of backgrounds and environments, with a chapter on the psychology of trading. Appendixes on program trading and portfolio insurance and options. Glossary.

The New Complete Guide to Environmental Careers. The Environmental Careers Organization. Island Press, Washington, DC, 1993.

> Provides an overview of the field, as well as chapters on specific areas of interest within the field. Includes interviews with professionals, job-search strategies, salary information, internship and volunteer ideas, and resource lists.

Occupational Outlook Handbook. U.S. Department of Labor, Bureau of Labor Statistics. Government Printing Office, Washington, DC, biennial.

> Describes in detail about 250 occupations. Keyed numerically to the *Dictionary of Occupational Titles*, this book describes the nature of the work, working conditions, training, employment outlook, earnings, and related occupations. Lists sources of additional information. Also available in CD-ROM format.

Paralegal: An Insider's Guide to One of the Fastest-Growing Occupations of the1990s, 2nd ed. Barbara Bernardo. Peterson's Guides, Princeton, NJ, 1993.
Describes the field, including issues and trends; lists professional associations, recruiters, and training programs. Bibliography.

Requirements for Certification of Teachers, Counselors, Librarians, Administrators for Elementary and Secondary Schools. John Tryneski, editor. The University of Chicago Press, Chicago, IL, annual.
Geographically arranged. The appendix lists addresses of state offices of certification.

VGM Careers for You Series. VGM Career Books, Lincolnwood, IL, 1991-1994.
Eighteen career guides aimed at ways of transforming various interests, skills, and avocations into careers.

VGM Professional Careers Series. VGM Career Books, Lincolnwood, IL, 1990-1994.
Separate volumes examine careers in accounting, advertising, business, child care, communications, computing, education, engineering, finance, government, health care, high tech, journalism, law, marketing, medicine, science, and social and rehabilitation services. A good way to gain an overview of the various positions and career paths within each field.

Organizational Culture

Companies That Care: The Most Family-Friendly Companies in America — What They Offer and How They Got That Way. Hal Morgan and Kerry Tucker. Simon & Schuster/Fireside, New York, NY, 1991.
The company profiles include information on child care, elder care, family leave, flexible work options, etc. Company size, state, and industry indexes.

The Insider's Guide to Law Firms, 2nd ed. Sheila V. Malkani and Michael F. Walsh, editors. Mobius Press, Boulder, CO, 1994.
Contains an introductory chapter on the hiring process, followed by geographically arranged profiles of over 200 firms. Each profile includes information on practice areas, training, pro bono work, structure, and hiring practices. Appendixes rank firms by: associates per partner; percentage of associates who make partner; percentage of pro bono work; percentage of women (partners and associates); percentage of minorities (partners and associates).

The 100 Best Companies for Gay Men and Lesbians. Ed Mickens. Pocket Books, New York, NY, 1994.
Introductory discussion of the issues facing gay men and lesbians in the

workplace, including a chapter on what businesses need to know. Profiles rate organizations "Excellent," "Good," or "Trying," and include information on lesbian and gay employee groups and domestic-partner benefits.

The 100 Best Companies to Work for in America. Robert Levering and Milton Moscowitz. Doubleday, New York, NY, 1993.
Alphabetically lists and describes the companies, rating them in terms of pay/benefits, opportunities, job security, pride in workplace/company, openness/fairness, and camaraderie/friendliness. Lists the biggest plus and biggest minus for each company, and ranks companies on just about any criterion you can think of. A lot of information!

Directories of Career Literature and Counselors

Books in Print. R.R. Bowker, New Providence, NJ, annual. Updated by *Books in Print Supplement* and *Forthcoming Books.*
The basic source of information concerning books offered for sale by distributors and publishers in the United States. Includes author and title listings. A separate, subject-classified *Subject Guide to Books in Print* lists career-relevant publications under Library of Congress subject headings. Also available in CD-ROM, microfiche, and online formats.

Business Information Sources, 3rd ed. Lorna M. Daniells. University of California Press, Berkeley, CA, 1993.
The first two chapters describe the types of libraries and general sources of information one is likely to consult. The rest of the book describes sources by business field or function. Subject and author/title indexes.

Directories in Print. Terri Kessler Schell, editor. Gale Research, Inc., Detroit, MI, biennial.
An annotated guide to over 15,000 directories published worldwide. Arranged in 26 major subject categories. Includes electronic and other formats. Alternative formats, subject, and title/keyword indexes. Also available online through DIALOG Information Sources, Inc. as part of the Gale Database of Publications and Broadcast Media (file 469).

Directory of Counseling Services. Nancy E. Roncketti, editor. International Association of Counseling Services, Inc., Alexandria, VA, annual.
Geographically lists the association's member organizations in the U.S. and Canada, including those at colleges and universities, and public and private agencies.

Gale Directory of Databases. Kathleen Lopez Nolan, editor. Gale Research Inc., Detroit, MI, semiannual. 2 volumes.

Volume one profiles online databases; volume two profiles CD-ROM, diskette, magnetic tape, handheld, and batch access database products. Sections on database producers, online services, and vendors/distributors. Geographic, subject, and master indexes. Also available online through ORBIT-QUESTEL and Data-Star and in CD-ROM format from Silver Platter Information, Inc.

National Directory of Certified Counselors. Victoria Wildermuth, editor. National Board for Certified Counselors, Greensboro, NC, 1994.
Geographic listing of certified counselors, career counselors, and clinical mental health counselors. Personal name index.

Directories of Trade and Professional Journals and Associations

Encyclopedia of Associations. Gale Research, Inc., Detroit, MI, annual. 3 volumes.
Volume 1 provides details on active nonprofit organizations of national scope, arranged in 18 subject categories, with name and keyword index. Volume 2 is a geographic and executive index to Volume 1. Volume 3 supplements Volume 1. A companion volume, *International Organizations*, describes international nonprofit membership organizations (including national organizations based outside of the U.S.), and includes geographic, executive, and name and keyword indexes. Also available in CD-ROM format and online through DIALOG Information Services, Inc. (file 114).

Gale Directory of Publications and Broadcast Media. Gale Research Inc., Detroit, MI, annual.
Geographically lists media, including newspapers, trade journals, radio and television stations, and cable systems in the U.S. and Canada, with cross-reference indexes for specific types of publications and radio station formats. Includes names, addresses, and telephone numbers of newspaper feature editors. Master name and keyword index.

Hudson's Subscription Newsletter Directory, 12th ed. Joan W. Artz, editor. Hudson's Subscription Newsletter Directory, Rhinebeck, NY, 1994.
Selective listings of subscription newsletters in the U.S. and abroad, by subject and geographic location. Title and editorial/publishing personnel indexes.

National Trade and Professional Associations of the United States. Columbia Books, Inc., Washington, DC, annual.
Lists trade associations, labor unions, and professional societies with national memberships. Subject, geographic, budget, executive, and acronym indexes. Includes a list of association management companies.

Standard Periodical Directory. Oxbridge Communications, Inc., New York, NY, annual.

A comprehensive subject listing of U.S. and Canadian periodicals, including consumer magazines, trade journals, directories, newsletters, house organs, yearbooks, etc. "Periodical," in this case, refers to any publication issued at least once every two years. Online and title indexes. Also available in CD-ROM format.

Ulrich's International Periodicals Directory. R.R. Bowker, New Providence, NJ, annual, with 3 supplements. 5 volumes.

A subject listing of over 140,000 serials from around the world. Indexes include: publications of international organizations, serials available on CD-ROM, serials available online, title, etc. Includes daily and weekly newspapers published in the U.S. Available online through DIALOG Information Services, Inc. and BRS Information Technologies, Inc., and in CD-ROM and microfiche formats.

Internships and Summer Work

The Access Guide to International Affairs Internships in the Washington, DC Area. Bruce Seymore II and Susan D. Krutt, editors. ACCESS: A Security Information Service, Washington, DC, 1994.

Lists opportunities with both government and nongovernmental organizations. Includes application and compensation information. Bibliography. Index of information strengths for the NGOs listed.

Directory of Financial Aids for Minorities. Gail Ann Schlachter and R. David Weber. Reference Service Press, San Carlos, CA, biennial.

Lists "scholarships, fellowships, loans, grants, awards, and internships designed primarily or exclusively for minorities." Annotated bibliography. Program title, sponsoring organization, geographic, subject, and calendar indexes.

Directory of Financial Aids for Women. Gail Ann Schlachter. Reference Service Press, San Carlos, CA, biennial.

Lists "scholarships, fellowships, loans, grants, awards, and internships designed primarily or exclusively for women." Annotated bibliography. Program title, sponsoring organization, geographic, subject, and calendar indexes.

Directory of Internships in Youth Development 1995: National Collaboration for Youth. The National Assembly of National Voluntary Health and Social Welfare Organizations, Washington, DC, 1995.

Geographically arranged internship listings include eligibility and contact information. An appendix lists awards and scholarships for service to communities.

GoodWorks: A Guide to Careers in Social Change, 5th ed. Donna Colvin, editor. Barricade Books, New York, NY, 1994.
Information on social change groups and internship and volunteer opportunities with them. Profiles individuals in the field and lists additional sources of information, as well as training programs. Geographic and topical indexes.

Jobs in Paradise: The Definitive Guide to Exotic Jobs Everywhere, revised ed. Jeffrey Maltzman. Harper Perennial, New York, NY, 1993.
Lists jobs in the U.S., Canada, the South Pacific, and the Caribbean by category: high adventure, mountains, tropical islands, snow & skiing, coasts & beaches, rivers, lakes, deserts, tour escorts, amusement & theme parks, cruise ships, and miscellaneous. Alphabetical and geographic employer indexes.

National Directory of Arts Internships. Warren Christensen and Steve Holt, editors. National Network for Artist Placement, Los Angeles, CA, biennial.
Listings in all areas of the arts. Introductory section on developing an internship, with practical advice on cover letters, resumes, portfolios, etc.

The National Directory of Internships. Garret D. Martin and Barbara E. Baker, editors. National Society for Internships and Experiential Education, Raleigh, NC, 1993.
Internships and fellowships arranged by type of organization. Alphabetical, geographic, and field indexes.

The New Careers Directory: Internships and Professional Opportunities in Technology and Social Change, 4th ed. Barry Lasky, editor. Student Pugwash USA, Washington, DC, 1993.
Profiles of organizations, including contact and hiring information. Contains advice for interns, annotated bibliography, and separate sections on international opportunities, and opportunities with the federal and state governments. Geographical and issue area indexes.

Peterson's Internships: Over 35,000 Opportunities to Get an Edge in Today's Competitive Job Market. Peterson's, Princeton, NJ, annual.
Includes contact and eligibility information for each listing, an introductory section on internships, and a list of internship referral and placement services. Field of interest, geographic, and employer indexes.

Peterson's Summer Opportunities for Kids and Teenagers. Peterson's, Princeton, NJ, annual.
Lists programs geographically, with a separate section of two-page descrip-

tions for some programs. Includes international listings, travel programs, a quick-reference chart of basic information, and a number of specialized indexes (special needs, religious affiliations, artistically talented, etc.). Many of the programs listed regularly hire college students to work for them. Alphabetical index of programs.

Summer Jobs USA. Peterson's, Princeton, NJ, annual.
Geographically arranged job listings, mostly at resorts, ranches, restaurants, lodgings, summer theaters, summer camps, and national parks. Most listings include the name of a contact person, salary information, and any fringe benefits. Includes a few Canadian listings and an introductory section on the summer job hunt. Category, employer, and job title indexes.

Summer Opportunities in Marine and Environmental Science: A Students' Guide to Jobs, Internships and Study, Camp and Travel Programs for High School and College Students, 2nd ed. Joy A. Herriott and Betty G. Herrin. Concord, MA, 1994.
Includes contact, eligibility, and compensation information. Resource list.

Summer Theatre Directory. Jill Charles, compiler and editor. Theatre Directories, Dorset, VT, annual.
Geographically arranged listings of theaters, theme parks, cruise line entertainment, and summer training programs, a few in Canada and London. Tips on auditioning and finding the "right" summer theater. Apprenticeship, internship, and employment information for performers, directors, designers, technicians, and managers. Alphabetical indexes of theaters and training programs.

Work and Study Abroad

Academic Year Abroad. Sara J. Steen, editor. Institute of International Education, New York, NY, annual.
Information on over 2,000 postsecondary study abroad programs that take place during the academic year. Geographic listings include deadline, credit, and cost information. Sponsoring institution, consortia, field of study, special option, and cost range indexes.

Adventure Holidays. Victoria Pybus, editor. Vacation-Work, Oxford, England, distributed by Peterson's Guides, Inc., Princeton, NJ, annual.
For those who want a focus to their travels, this book is a good place to look. Programs are listed geographically within each activity; features such pursuits as cycling and research expeditions. Index of companies and organizations.

The Almanac of International Jobs and Careers: A Guide to Over 1001

Employers, 2nd ed. Ronald L. Krannich and Caryl Rae Krannich. Impact Publications, Manassas Park, VA, 1994.
> Introductory chapter, followed by listings of employers by category. Includes a chapter on internships, volunteer programs, and study abroad. Resource lists. Subject, employer, and resource indexes.

Alternatives to the Peace Corps: A Directory of Third World and U.S. Volunteer Opportunities. Annette Olson, editor. Food First, Oakland, CA, 1994.
> Introductory information, followed by listings of international and U.S. voluntary service organizations, study tours, and alternative travel groups. Resource lists. Index of organizations.

American Jobs Abroad. Victoria Harlow and Edward W. Knappman, editors. Gale Research Inc., Detroit, MI, biennial.
> Information on securing employment abroad, making the move, and living abroad; descriptions of U.S. corporations, government agencies, and other not-for-profit organizations that employ Americans overseas; country profiles. Job category index.

China Bound: A Guide to Academic Life and Work in the PRC. Anne F. Thurston with Karen Turner-Gottschang and Linda A. Reed. National Academy Press, Washington, DC, 1994.
> Written for the Committee on Scholarly Communication with China, this book discusses practical issues from passports and visas, to quality of life once there. Resource lists. Indexed.

Commonwealth Universities Yearbook. Association of Commonwealth Universities, London, England, annual.
> Geographically arranged information on Commonwealth institutions. Institution and organization, field of study, and name indexes.

Current Research in Britain. The British Library, West Yorkshire, England. Separate annual volumes for physical sciences, biological sciences, and social sciences; biennial humanities volume.
> Lists research in progress by institution. Name, study area, and keyword indexes.

Directory of American Firms Operating in Foreign Countries, 13th ed. World Trade Academy Press. Uniworld Business Publications, Inc., New York, NY, 1994. 3 volumes.
> Volume One contains alphabetical listings of U.S. firms operating overseas providing, in some cases, names of the president/CEO, chief foreign officer, and personnel director. Volumes Two and Three index firms by country, and include name and U.S. address of parent firm as well as name and address of subsidiary or affiliate in that country.

Directory of Foreign Firms Operating in the United States, 7th ed. World Trade Academy Press. Uniworld Business Publications, Inc., New York, NY, 1992.
> Firms grouped by country, listing their American affiliates. Foreign firm and American affiliate indexes.

Directory of U.S. International Health Organizations. The National Council for International Health, Washington, DC, 1992.
> Alphabetical listing of organizations. Lists contacts, activities, publications, etc. Activity and country indexes.

Emplois D'Eté en France. Francois Armen. VAC-JOB, Paris, France, annual.
> Organized both geographically and by type of job. Chapters on au pair arrangements, boarding and lodging, and information for foreign students. In French.

Financial Aid for Research and Creative Activities Abroad. Gail Ann Schlachter and R. David Weber. Reference Service Press, San Carlos, CA, biennial.
> Lists scholarships, fellowships, loans, grants, awards, and internships for high school/undergraduate students, graduate students, postdocs, and professionals/other individuals. Annotated bibliography. Program, sponsoring organization, geographic, subject, and deadline indexes.

Financial Aid for Study and Training Abroad. Gail Ann Schlachter and R. David Weber. Reference Service Press, San Carlos, CA, biennial.
> Lists scholarships, fellowships, loans, grants, awards, and internships for high school/undergraduate students, graduate students, postdocs, and professionals/other individuals. Annotated bibliography. Program, sponsoring organization, geographic, subject, and deadline indexes.

Ford's Freighter Travel Guide...and waterways of the world. Ford's Travel Guides, Northridge, CA, semiannual.
> Arranged by port or waterway, lists schedules and itineraries of freighters that carry passengers. Includes listings of travel agents, foreign government tourist offices, sports and casual cruises, and ferry lines. Index of steamship lines.

Ford's International Cruise Guide. Ford's Travel Guides, Northridge, CA, quarterly.
> Complete schedules for approximately 200 ships. Cruise ship, cruise line, and geographic indexes.

The Guide to Academic Travel, 2nd ed. ShawGuides, Inc., Coral Gables, FL, 1992.
> "Adult study and language vacations sponsored by colleges, museums, & educational organizations." Geographic, specialty, and master indexes.

The Harvard Guide to International Experience. William G. Klingelhofer.

Office of Career Services, Faculty of Arts and Sciences, Harvard University, Cambridge, MA, 1989.
> Chapters on preparing to go abroad, study abroad, work abroad, volunteering abroad, and funding the international experience, each with its own bibliography.

InterAction Member Profiles. The American Council for Voluntary International Action, Washington, DC, 1991.
> Information on private and voluntary organizations dedicated to international humanitarian issues. Includes program, personnel, finance, and publication data for most listings. Program, geographic, and personnel indexes.

International Corporate Yellow Book: Who's Who at the Leading Non-U.S. Companies. Monitor Leadership Directories, Inc., New York, NY, semiannual.
> Company listings by region; parent company, U.S. subsidiary, geographic, industry, and individual's name indexes. Time zone and world holiday charts. Also available in CD-ROM format.

International Handbook of Universities. The International Association of Universities. Stockton Press, New York, NY, biennial.
> Geographic listing of basic information on university-level degree-granting institutions around the world.

International Internships and Volunteer Programs: International Options for Students and Professionals. Will Cantrell and Francine Modderno. Worldwise Books, Oakton, VA, 1992.
> Five sections: government/international organizations, academic programs, independent internships/traineeships, volunteer opportunities with private organizations, and miscellaneous work opportunities.

International Jobs: Where They Are and How to Get Them, 4th ed. Eric Kocher. Addison-Wesley Publishing Co., Reading, MA, 1993.
> Part one, "International Career Planning and Job Strategy," covers the process of getting a job. Part two, "The International Job Market," profiles employers across a range of fields, from the federal government through teaching and international law. Bibliography. Index.

International Research Centers Directory. Thomas J. Cochonski, editor. Gale Research Inc., Detroit, MI, biennial.
> Multinational section, followed by listings by country. Subject, country, and keyword indexes. Also available online through DIALOG Information Services, Inc.

International Travel Health Guide. Stuart R. Rose. Travel Medicine, Inc., Northampton, MA, annual.

Discusses trip preparation and strategies for avoiding disease while traveling. Includes regional disease risk summaries, country-by-country health advisories, a list of air ambulance companies worldwide, and a list of travelers' clinics in the United States and Canada.

Invest Yourself: The Catalogue of Volunteer Opportunities: A Guide to Action. Susan G. Angus, editorial coordinator. The Commission on Voluntary Service and Action, Inc., New York, NY, 1993.
Alphabetical listings of agencies, with indexes indicating full-time/part-time and international/intercultural opportunities, as well as work camps, categories of skills and interests needed, and program location.

The ISS Directory of Overseas Schools: The Comprehensive Guide to K-12 American and International Schools Worldwide. International Schools Services, Princeton, NJ, annual.
Geographically arranged profiles of schools. Indexes of schools offering the international baccalaureate and schools with boarding facilities. Lists accrediting associations and regional and international organizations.

Jobs in Japan, 4th ed. John Wharton. The Global Press, Rockville, MD, 1991.
A combination how-to and where-to survival guide. Listings of private English-language schools.

Let's Go Travel Guides. St. Martin's Press, New York, NY, annual.
Budget travel guides, researched and written by students for Harvard Student Agencies, which provide practical travel advice and ideas for exploration of various geographic locales.

Living in China: A Guide to Teaching and Studying in China Including Taiwan. Rebecca Weiner, et al. China Books & Periodicals, Inc., San Francisco, CA, 1991.
Includes chapters on packing, adjusting to the culture, and travel in China. Directories of schools, teaching organizations, and student programs. Appendixes on the Chinese language, publications, China-related resource organizations, and key universities in China.

Money for International Exchange in the Arts. James M. Gullong and Noreen Tomassi, editors. American Council for the Arts, New York, NY, 1992.
Published in association with Arts International. Lists service organizations, foundations, corporations, international contacts, and government agencies that provide support for artists and arts organizations. Organization, geographic, discipline, and type of support indexes.

Overseas Summer Jobs. David Woodworth, editor. Vacation-Work, Oxford, England, distributed by Peterson's Guides, Inc., Princeton, NJ, annual.
Geographic arrangement of summer employment opportunities; includes

volunteer work. Visa, residence, and work regulation information. Separate chapter on au pairs, paying guests, and exchange visits.

The Peace Corps and More: 120 Ways to Work, Study and Travel in the Third World. Medea Benjamin. Global Exchange, San Francisco, CA, 1993.
Basic information on planning Third World experiences, as well as profiles of organizations. Bibliography.

Peterson's Study Abroad: A Guide to Semester and Yearlong Academic Programs. Peterson's, Princeton, NJ, annual.
Includes general information on study abroad, as well as a list of tour programs. Geographic listings of study abroad programs include eligibility and cost information. Field of study, program sponsor, host institution, and enrollment facilitator indexes.

Russia Survival Guide: The Definitive Guide to Doing Business & Traveling in Russia, 5th ed. Paul E. Richardson. Russian Information Services, Montpelier, VT, 1994.
Chapters on trip preparations, travel/accommodations, money/crime, food/health, communication, doing business, and Russian business law. Provides country background information, including lists of published and online services. Indexed.

The Safe Travel Book, revised ed. Peter Savage. Lexington Books, New York, NY, 1993.
Discusses health and security issues for travelers, including the trip home and arrival in the U.S. Includes a time line to departure date, keyed to information in the rest of the book.

Smart Vacations: The Traveler's Guide to Learning Adventures Abroad. Priscilla Tovey, editor. Council on International Educational Exchange. St. Martin's Press, New York, NY, 1993.
Contains information on study tours, outdoor adventures, archaeological digs, art programs, language study, and voluntary service. Location, program type, and general indexes.

Staying Healthy in Asia, Africa, and Latin America. Dirk G. Schroeder. Moon Publications, Inc., Chico, CA, 1993.
Discusses prevention, diagnosis, and treatment of illnesses and first-aid emergencies. Bibliography. Indexed.

Study Abroad. UNESCO. Paris, France, triennial.
Describes international study programs offered by institutions in over 125 countries, with a section devoted to financial assistance. International organization, institution, and subject of study indexes. In English, French, and Spanish.

Summer Jobs Britain. David Woodworth, editor. Vacation Work, Oxford, England, distributed by Peterson's Guides, Inc., Princeton, NJ, annual.

Arranged geographically and topically; includes volunteer work. Includes a chapter on au pair, home help, and paying guest opportunities.

Teaching EFL Outside the United States. Gary Butzback, et al., editors. TESOL, Inc., Alexandria, VA, 1993.

Country profiles describing qualifications and requirements for teaching EFL, nationality restrictions, working conditions, etc. Includes some school, organization, and contact information. Resource lists for some countries. List of job placement and referral teacher exchanges.

Teaching English Abroad. Susan Griffith. Vacation Work, Oxford, England, distributed by Peterson's Guides, Inc., Princeton, NJ, 1994.

Information on training, finding a job, preparation, etc. Country-by-country guide to securing teaching employment for both qualified and unqualified teachers.

The Underground Guide to University Study in Britain and Ireland. Bill Griesar. Intercultural Press, Inc., Yarmouth, ME, 1992.

Discusses a range of issues relevant to living and studying in Britain and Ireland, from choosing an academic program to social/cultural issues. Appendixes list resources, universities, vocabulary, and calendar and travel information.

Vacation Study Abroad. Sara J. Steen, editor. Institute of International Education, New York, NY, annual.

Provides information on over 1,500 summer programs and on short courses in the fall, winter, or spring. Lists both U.S.- and foreign-sponsored programs. Geographic listings include deadline, credit, and cost information. Sponsoring institution, consortia, field of study, special option, cost range, and duration indexes.

Volunteer! The Comprehensive Guide to Voluntary Service in the U.S. and Abroad, 1992-1993 ed. Max Terry, editor. Council on International Educational Exchange and Council of Religious Volunteer Agencies, New York, NY, 1992.

Basic information on voluntary service followed by short-term and medium/long-term project listings. Organization/publication, skills, and program location indexes. Includes essays by former volunteers.

Volunteer Vacations: Short-Term Adventures That Will Benefit You and Others, 4th ed. Bill McMillon. Chicago Review Press, Chicago, IL, 1993.

Profiles sponsoring organizations, including cost and application information. Section of volunteer vignettes. Cost, length, location, season, and type indexes. Bibliography.

Work, Study, Travel Abroad: The Whole World Handbook. Council on International Educational Exchange. St. Martin's Press, New York, NY, biennial.

> This publication is packed with information and advice on work and study abroad, with numerous references to other sources of information. Geographically arranged.

Work Your Way Around the World. Susan Griffith. Vacation Work, Oxford, England, distributed by Peterson's Guides, Inc., Princeton, NJ, biennial.

> Introductory information on work and travel, with advice and suggestions. Sections on different types of work, as well as geographic listing of employment opportunities. Includes a section on voluntary work.

World Chamber of Commerce Directory. Loveland, CO, annual.

> Lists U.S. and Canadian chambers of commerce geographically. Includes state boards of tourism, convention and visitor bureaus, and economic development organizations in the U.S., as well as American chambers of commerce abroad, foreign tourist information bureaus, and foreign chambers of commerce in the U.S. A separate section provides listings for the U.S. Congress, dean of diplomatic corps, foreign embassies in the U.S., and U.S. embassies.

The World Factbook. U.S. Central Intelligence Agency. Brassey's, Washington, DC, annual.

> Country profiles, providing information on geography, people, government, economy, communications, and defense forces. Appendixes include information on the United Nations and other international groups and a cross-reference list of geographic names.

The World of Learning. Europa Publications Limited, London, England, annual.

> Geographic arrangement of educational institutions, libraries, learned societies, and scientific and cultural organizations. Separate section on international organizations. Index of institutions.

Worldwide Government Directory with International Organizations. Belmont Publications, Bethesda, MD, annual.

> Part I is arranged by country and outlines the governmental structure, including the legislative and the judicial, as well as the central bank, United Nations mission, and major foreign embassies located in the country. Part II lists international organizations alphabetically, including UN organizations, agencies, commissions, etc.

Chapter 3

CAREER DECISION MAKING

INTRODUCTION

Developing your career requires making decisions. Planning the expertise that you want to develop and the kind of work you want to be doing involves making choices. The clearer you are about the skills and knowledge that you want to develop, the easier it is to make decisions about jobs and graduate study. Likewise, the more certain you are about what type of work you want to contribute to, the easier it is to plan your next move.

Setting goals for the development of your expertise will be ongoing throughout your life. You may want to think in terms of five-year plans. In developing these plans, you will want to assess what expertise you have that you want to expand. You will also want to make predictions, based on the information you have been gathering, about what expertise will be required for accomplishing work in your preferred field or what will be the most transferable, allowing you to move from one field to another.

Choosing the career field to which you would like to contribute your energy and talents will help to provide focus to your planning. Through your career exploration you have the opportunity to gain insight into the rewards and satisfactions in various career fields. Since one can use the same expertise in many different fields, your decision about which career field to work in can be based on which one will be most energizing and rewarding to you. This is a decision you will be reviewing periodically.

Preparing for the Changing Job Market

Two additional factors to consider in making career decisions are the development of your professional reputation and your proficiency in dealing with change. Your professional reputation is based on your demonstrated skills and knowledge and your record of accomplishments. Now that employers can no longer guarantee long-term employment, the individual must maximize his own employability by continually expanding his skills and adding to his record of accomplishments. An employer faced with a new project looks around for the person who has a reputation for getting things done. It is the quality of your relevant experience and past accomplishments, more than the name of your former employers, that will attract the attention of your next employer and help you secure your next job.

No matter what career field you choose and what expertise you develop, it is certain that you will have to cope with change. There may be times when you continue in the same job, but have to change completely how you get your work done or even what work you do. On the other hand, you may have to change jobs because your expertise is no longer needed or your position disappears. Change may be predictable or it may come as a surprise. With global competition and developing technology to cope with, employers need workers who have a positive attitude toward change, i.e., who become more productive when faced with change rather than less productive. You can increase your proficiency in dealing with change through experience. During college and the early years of your career, it is wise to develop your "change skills." Especially if you have a tendency to view change as stressful rather than energizing, sign up for college activities, part-time work, or summer jobs that require you to deal with new situations and people.

Another aspect of career decision making is the balancing of your investment of time and energy in your career life and in your personal life. Your goals for this balance may be different from one stage of your life to the next, but the issue will always be on the agenda.

PREPARING FOR CAREER DECISIONS

Developing Your Own Style

Whether you are deciding about your career field or choosing your summer job, there is no one right way to make decisions. Different individuals make their career decisions differently. The balance between the assessment of available facts, advice from significant others, personal reflection, and your intuitive sense will vary from one person to another, and may change with a particular individual from one decision to the next. When a decision seems important, you may hesitate to trust your intuition. However, because it is not possible to know all the facts about yourself or a career opportunity, your intuition may be an important guide.

No matter what your decision-making style, becoming well informed improves the quality of your decisions. Getting to know yourself—your values, interests, and abilities—helps you make decisions about what expertise you want to develop and what accomplishments will be meaningful to you.

Increasing Your Self-Knowledge

Being able to describe your strengths, preferences, and goals is fundamental to managing your career development. Becoming aware of and learning to express what your special talents are, what you find exciting, and what you find rewarding is an important component of career decision making. This requires that you continue to be analytical about your experiences as was discussed in Chapter 2.

As you gather information by visiting career advisers at work and by arranging short-term work experiences, see if you can identify with the people you meet. How are you like them? How are you different? Could you do what they do if you had the appropriate training? Would you enjoy doing what they do? Do you share similar values and goals?

Some people find that vocational interest tests assist them in developing self-knowledge. The data that you provide on these inventories are analyzed to generate an interest profile which is matched with the profile of people in a variety of occupations. From these occupational matches, you may derive insight into what job characteristics are important to you.

Some people find that self-assessment exercises help them to increase their self-knowledge. Exercises can bring into conscious awareness your preferred activities, interests, and values and give you the opportunity to think about them objectively. Try the exercises in Chapter 2 to get started and if you want more, consult the books listed in the bibliography at the end of this chapter.

Tests and exercises, however, cannot do the work for you. You must learn to be analytical about your experiences and to trust your own perception of your strengths, preferences, and values.

Keeping Your Options Open

If you do not feel ready to make a commitment that structures your options for the future, such as going to medical school or law school, it is very possible to plan employment that provides the opportunity to work with professionals in the field to learn more about their work and to discover what they find rewarding.

While you are deliberating about the choice of your first career field, you may want to take a job that is related to your leading career option, or you may want to arrange an experience that is completely different from it. Sometimes an adventure working abroad for a year or two or exploring an avocational interest helps you to clarify your long-range goals.

LIVING WITH INDECISION

You are living in a society that is very career-oriented. Since you were very young, people have been asking you, "What are you going to be when you grow up?" What was your answer? How did you feel about it? Now that you are grown-up, how do you answer this question? You may be undecided about your career direction because of a lack of information about yourself and what you want in your career, or because you do not want to make a commitment to a specific field at this time. Whatever the source of your indecision, you need to accept and learn to live with it. The following are some of the strategies students have developed for living with indecision.

- Take a short-term view of your planning. Commit yourself wholeheartedly to your current educational endeavors: be the best English or biology scholar that you can be. Learn as much as you can and develop your reading and writing skills. Make the most of the intellectual and educational resources that you have around you.

- Enter into college or community activities. Focus on making the institution a better place, or take part in community work. Help make life a little better for those who are less fortunate than you by serving as a volunteer.

- Collect new experiences. Seek interesting and preferably different experiences every summer and year that you are in college. Live fully in the present. This approach to your college experience will give you information which will help you make career choices when you are ready to think about the future and will be an investment in the development of your skills.

- Take on a different career identity each semester or year. When you are trying out a particular career identity, visit people who are in that career, read what they read, and arrange work experiences which will bring you into contact with them. This will enable you to wear that career label knowledgeably and seriously. When people ask you about your plans, answer with whatever your tentative career identity is. You will quickly learn what their particular evaluations of that career are. Trying on a different identity each semester will give you the opportunity to experience how that role feels. It will be an interesting adventure and it will broaden your knowledge about the opportunities available to you.

If you are undecided because there are two or three fields that you are interested in, explore the possibility of pursuing two careers at one time. Or perhaps you can integrate two fields of work into one career. Rather than forcing yourself to give up one of two alternatives that interest you, explore the possibility of pursuing them sequentially. In this case, you will only have to decide which to pursue first.

One of the best ways to live with indecision in this career-oriented society is to begin a planned program of career exploration. Visiting career advisers who themselves experienced long years of indecision can be a validation of your current state of mind. Having experiences that prove there are interesting alternatives that you might pursue is also reassuring. As you engage in career exploration, it may be helpful for you to set target dates by which you hope to make a tentative decision about the career in which you plan to work after graduation.

Keep in mind that you are not looking for the perfect lifetime job. You are looking for an opportunity to learn more about yourself, to increase your job skills, and to explore a particular work environment. There is no "wrong" first job if you learn something from the experience.

MOVING FROM ONE CAREER FIELD TO ANOTHER

Increasing numbers of people are working in more than one career field during their lifetime. Sometimes these changes are made only in one direction; other times an individual may spend a few years in a second career field and then move back to his original career. Sometimes these moves are planned years in advance; other times they are unanticipated and are undertaken because of adverse events or lack of satisfaction in the first field. Sometimes these moves require returning to graduate school.

A change of career field is usually stimulating and leads to a marked increase in productivity, as well as increased satisfaction and self-worth. A new career field provides opportunities for different modes of self-expression, changed relationships with people, and new contributions to the community. Changing careers allows you to expand your range of accomplishments, experience new kinds of rewards, and develop new talents.

Working in multiple career fields may be part of your plans from the beginning. When developing your career goals, you may decide that you want to develop expertise that is fungible, i.e., that will be useful in several career fields. For example, you might spend the early years of your career in banking with the idea that at some time you would like to move into university administration as a financial officer. Or, you might work as a reporter on a daily newspaper and then become a press officer for a member of Congress. In these moves, it is obvious that the skills learned in the first career are preparation for the second one.

On the other hand, you may decide to make a career change because you are no longer enjoying your current work or you are not achieving the kinds of opportunities that you had hoped for, or because you seek new challenges. In this case you might become interested in moving to a career field that is very different from your present work and, therefore, the relevance of your current skills and knowledge is not easily discernible.

Exploring New Career Fields

From newspapers and television, and from staying in touch with your network of professional friends, you will be continually gathering information about developments in your own career field and other fields in which you have some interest. When you are thinking about making a change, you should intensify your information gathering. Start by reading what professionals in the field read. This will introduce you to the issues and problems that they think about. Reading is a convenient way to get started and can be done in your personal time.

Interviewing people at work and experiencing the environment in which they work will be an essential part of your career search. It is best to interview both people who are in their early years in a particular field and established people, in order to gain a variety of perspectives on career opportunities.

If you are employed full-time in your current work, you may have to meet with people outside of their working hours. This will limit the possibilities of getting a feeling for their daily work and environment. Before you make a decision about a new field, it may be advisable to take time off from your current job, so that you can experience the potential new work environment.

The activities and lifestyles may be very different from those you have been experiencing in your current career. Give yourself time to experiment with this different career identity. Arrange to spend time at work with someone in your targeted field so that you can test yourself in the new environment. How does it feel? Does the work seem interesting to you? What do these people find rewarding in their work?

Translating Your Skills

Don't restrict your exploration of potential career fields because of concerns about the applicability of your skills. First of all, as a college graduate with some years of work experience, you have many important work skills. Employers value intellectual, analytical, communication, language, computer, and interpersonal skills, all of which you have been developing. The discussion of work attributes in the section Presenting Yourself on the job market in Chapter 4 provides questions which will help you increase your awareness of your general work skills. As you research career options and learn about the work people do in each field, you will gain new insights and vocabulary for assessing and translating your skills.

Secondly, some of your specific job skills may be useful in ways that you will only understand as you learn more about the career field. For one thing, you may find that your skills have a different name. Every field has its own jargon, and you will learn that jargon from your reading and conversations with career advisers. As a career changer, it is your responsibility to be able to describe your talents and skills in their language. Using their language communicates the message that you have researched their field and that you will fit in.

If you find that there are specific job skills that you must have to be competitive in your next career, research the ways that you might develop them. In order to acquire certain skills and credentials, you may need to enter graduate school; for example, if you want to be in the legal professions, you need to earn a law degree. But for many types of career moves, you will be able to demonstrate that you have the talents required through your volunteer work or through taking on extra responsibilities in your current work. For example, if you are interested in public relations, offer to do public relations for a community organization. Sometimes taking a few evening courses is sufficient to learn the language and skills of your next career field.

Finding Support in Your Network

Find somebody who will listen to you as you assess the pluses and minuses of the career fields you are exploring and contrast them with your present situation. You are seeking a friend, a spouse, a professional colleague, or a career counselor—preferably somebody who does not have preconceived notions of what you should be—to listen to you and ask you questions to help you clarify the feelings that you are having as you plan this move. The choice of your new career will be yours alone, but having someone to whom you can relate your experiences, and with whom you can examine your reactions to those experiences, can be very supportive and productive.

Although the prospect of making a change may seem difficult, the challenges and opportunities of new responsibilities will add richness and diversity to your life.

CONSIDERING GRADUATE STUDY

As you learn about the world of work and assess your talents and interests in relation to the opportunities you find, you may choose a career goal that requires a graduate degree. It is not possible to be a lawyer without completing law school, it is not possible to be a doctor without completing medical school, and if you want to pursue an academic career, you will need to earn a Ph.D.

Before you commit yourself to a career goal that requires a graduate or professional degree, it is best to spend time with professionals in several different areas in that field. Although you cannot engage in actual practice in most professions before earning the required degree, it is possible to work closely with professionals and experience vicariously the opportunities, demands, and rewards of their work.

You may also decide to go to graduate school after years of working as a way to change careers or to enhance your credentials and opportunities in the field that you have been working in. Returning to school to earn a graduate degree in mid-life is scary and sometimes difficult to arrange, but most people find it stimulating and rewarding.

An Introduction to Three Professions

There are many career fields in which advanced professional study is required or preferred: for example, architecture, business, theology, education, engineering, international relations, library and information science, mental health, and public policy. Selected references to assist you in beginning your exploration of these fields are listed in the Index of Resources by Career Field at the back of this book. In this section we will discuss briefly only three professions: academe, law, and medicine.

Academe

If you are reading this book while you are a college student, you have probably been in school all your life. If you have enjoyed your academic work and have done well, you may be thinking about academe as one of your career options.

Intellectual curiosity, enthusiasm for a specific field of study, and interest in independent inquiry are important factors in choosing an academic career. The central challenges in a career on the faculty of a college or university are expanding the boundaries of knowledge; identifying questions and seeking the answers; communicating your ideas through writing, speaking, and publishing; and sharing your knowledge with students. Teaching is an integral part of the search for fuller understanding of the fundamental concepts and structure of your field. Interaction with students often generates new questions and insights.

If you are a college student, becoming involved in research with a professor in your major field of interest will enrich your education. It will also give you the opportunity to find out whether you enjoy doing research. Reviewing the literature for your research papers will introduce you to various areas of study in the field. You may have already had teaching experience as a tutor, a teaching assistant in high school or college, or a friend to whom others come for assistance. Research and teaching introduce you to the activities of an academic career, but getting to know your professors well so that you can understand the satisfactions and rewards that they find in their careers will be most helpful in deciding whether you want to undertake a Ph.D. program.

Law

Lawyers take the role of advocate, negotiator, and adversary in their function as intermediaries between the law and the people. Whether his client is the government, a corporation, or an individual, a lawyer is responsible for interpreting the law to his client and for providing counsel on the legal issues related to specific decisions. The lawyer may initiate legal action on behalf of his client or undertake his client's defense if the client is accused of an illegal act. Lawyers in private practice assist individuals and organizations in understanding their rights and privileges within the law. Lawyers in public interest organizations work through the courts, the government, and the media to promote civil rights, arms control, protection of the environment, or whatever their issues are. Lawyers working for the government have many responsibilities: legislation, interpretation, administration, and litigation.

The practice of law requires excellence in written and oral expression. Lawyers do a great deal of writing: the preparation of briefs which present a detailed defense of the client's position; the development of regulations for the implementation of legislation; the preparation of contracts, partnerships, wills, trusts, and other legal documents. Lawyers must be articulate in instructing their clients about the law, litigating cases in court, and negotiating disputes.

Many kinds of work experience can give you insight into the legal profession. Doing research as a paralegal provides the opportunity to work on legal problems, but so do many jobs for college graduates in the executive, legislative, or judicial branches of federal, state, or local government. Talking to lawyers in different types of practice will help you survey the variety of career opportunities in the field, as will books like *Choosing a Career in the Law* and *Careers in International Law*, listed in the bibliography at the end of Chapter 2. Reading publications such as *The National Law Journal* or the *ABA Journal* will give you a sense of what topics are important to lawyers.

Medicine

Medicine is a science-based helping profession. The basic responsibility of the physician is to treat people who are ill or in pain and to help people maintain good health. Most doctors spend all of their professional time seeing patients; some of their personal time is spent this way as well, when they respond to emergency calls. Some doctors conduct medical research and teach medical students and residents, but they may also take care of patients.

There are many different specialties in medicine and many types of practice. The patients, the medical problems, the treatment modalities, and the patient interaction differ widely between psychiatry and surgery, geriatrics and pediatrics. Choice of specialty is usually made during medical school, after clinical clerkships in each major specialty.

Increasingly, doctors are practicing in clinics, health maintenance organizations, and other types of group practice. The number of physicians in private practice is expected to decrease steadily in the foreseeable future.

Spending time with a doctor while he is taking care of patients or making rounds, working with patients in a hospital as a volunteer or in a paid job, or being a research assistant on a medical research project are all ways to learn about the profession of medicine. Essays in *The Harvard College Premedical Guide* by practicing physicians provide insiders' views of the field. Medical journals such as *American Medical News* are excellent sources of information on the important issues in the profession.

Other health fields that you may want to explore include dentistry, nursing, public health, and health policy and administration. The *Occupational Outlook Handbook* briefly describes these professions and their graduate study requirements. The VGM Professional Careers Series will also introduce you to a variety of health care career options.

Taking the First Step

As you can see from the examples of academe, law, and medicine, the exploration process for career fields requiring advanced study follows the same pattern as that described in Chapter 2: reading the literature, interviewing and observing practitioners, and gaining related paid or unpaid work experience. Ask yourself the same questions with regard to your personal preferences and priorities, relating them to the characteristics of the profession you are considering. Try to arrange opportunities to spend time with professionals in the field.

To get started, you might consult the Index of Resources by Career Field at the end of this book. For financial aid and graduate and professional school information, consult the resources listed in the Graduate and Professional Education and Financial Aid and Grants sections of the bibliography at the end of this chapter.

SOURCES

Self-Assessment

Career Planning Today, 3rd ed. C. Randall Powell. Kendall/Hunt Publishing Company, Dubuque, IA, 1995.
> A comprehensive look at the process of career planning, from self-assessment to job search to career advancement. The "Guide to Selected Topics" provides a good overview of the material.

Outside the Ivory Tower: A Guide for Academics Considering Alternative Careers. Margaret Newhouse. Office of Career Services, Faculty of Arts and Sciences, Harvard University, Cambridge, MA, 1993.
> Although geared toward graduate students, anyone could benefit from the self-assessment exercises in Chapter 1, as well as the "mini-tour" of nonacademic careers in Chapter 3. Annotated bibliography.

Self-Assessment and Career Development, 3rd ed. James G. Clawson et al. Prentice-Hall, Englewood Cliffs, NJ, 1992.
> Stresses self-assessment in combination with career, job, and lifestyle planning. Includes case studies, exercises, and resource lists.

Street-Smart Career Guide: A Step-by-Step Program for Your Career Development. Laura Pedersen. Crown Trade Paperbacks, New York, NY, 1993.
> Discusses career planning for tomorrow's marketplace, as well as the mechanics of searching for and securing employment. Bibliography.

What Color Is Your Parachute? A Practical Manual for Job-Hunters and Career Changers. Richard Nelson Bolles. Ten Speed Press, Berkeley, CA, annual.
> Chapters on job hunting and interviewing, with emphasis on exercises as a means of self-evaluation. Lists additional sources of information on careers and job hunting. Indexed.

Workstyles to Fit Your Lifestyle: Everyone's Guide to Temporary Employment. John Fanning and Rosemary Maniscalco. Prentice-Hall, Englewood Cliffs, NJ, 1993.
> Discusses the decision to seek temporary employment, as well as the skills desirable in specific fields. Includes chapters on advancement within a temporary service, temping as a means to permanent employment, transitional temping, etc.

Graduate and Professional Education

AAA Guide: A Guide to Departments/A Directory of Members. American Anthropological Association. Arlington, VA, annual.
> Profiles anthropology departments in colleges and universities, museums, research institutions, and government. Includes statistics on students and degree holders and a list of dissertations submitted during the year. Name and department indexes.

Admission Requirements of U.S. and Canadian Dental Schools. American Association of Dental Schools. Washington, DC, annual.
> Discusses dentistry as a career, the dental school application process, and funding for dental education. Profiles dental schools, including admissions, curriculum, and financial information.

The AWP Official Guide to Writing Programs. D.W. Fenza and Beth Jarock, editors. Associated Writing Programs, Old Dominion University, Norfolk, VA, biennial.
> Profiles writing programs and their faculty in the U.S., Canada, and the United Kingdom; also describes writers' centers, colonies, and conferences. Geographic and degree indexes.

Directory of Graduate Programs. Graduate Record Examinations Board and the Council of Graduate Schools. Educational Testing Service, Princeton, NJ, biennial. 4 volumes.
> Tabular arrangement of U.S. graduate program information, including size of faculty and student body, degrees offered, admission requirements, and financial aid options. Supplemental information in narrative form arranged geographically.

Directory of Professional Programs in TESOL in the United States 1992-1994. Helen Kornblum with Ellen Garshick. Teachers of English to Speakers of Other Languages, Inc., Alexandria, VA, 1992.
> Provides basic information about college and university certificate and degree programs. Includes state certification requirements. Geographic index.

Directory of Theatre Training Programs. Jill Charles, compiler and editor. Theatre Directories, Dorset, VT, biennial.
> Introductory articles on theater training, followed by geographic listings of mostly U.S. college and conservatory programs. Includes information on admissions, degrees offered, faculty, courses, facilities, productions, and philosophy of training. Alphabetical index of institutions.

Educational Opportunities of Greater Boston for Adults: A Comprehensive Directory of Day and Evening Classes. The Educational Resource Institute (TERI), Boston, MA, annual.
> Lists adult and continuing education courses throughout the metropolitan Boston area; includes schedules and costs.

The Electronic University: A Guide to Distance Learning. Published in cooperation with National University Continuing Education Association. Peterson's Guides, Princeton, NJ, 1993.
> Alphabetical profiles of institutions offering courses and degree programs at a distance. Includes a glossary and list of consortia/networks. Geographic and subject indexes.

Getting In: A Step-by-Step Plan for Gaining Admission to Graduate School in Psychology. American Psychological Association. Washington, DC, 1993.
> Includes chapters on the decision to apply, choice of program, evaluation criteria used by schools, the application process, accepting and declining offers, and alternatives if not accepted. Includes a resource list, timetable, and sample recommendation form.

Getting into Law School Today. Thomas H. Martinson and David P. Waldherr. Prentice Hall, New York, NY, 1994.
> Chapters on the structure of legal education in the United States, the admissions process, the law school application, the personal statement,

and the LSAT. Includes sample personal statements, guidelines for recommenders, and a list of ABA-accredited schools.

Graduate Study in Psychology. American Psychological Association, Inc. Washington, DC, annual.

Four sections: departments and schools of psychology offering the doctoral degree; other departments offering the doctoral degree; graduate departments of psychology offering less than the doctoral degree; other graduate departments offering less than the doctoral degree. Area of study and institution indexes.

Guide to Arts Administration Training. Center for Arts Administration, Graduate School of Business, University of Wisconsin-Madison and Association of Arts Administration Educators. ACA Books, New York, NY, biennial.

Profiles programs in the U.S. and Canada. Includes lists of seminars, workshops, institutes, and job-listing services.

Guide to Graduate Education in Urban and Regional Planning, 8th ed. Ved Prakash and Victor A. Brusi Amador, editors. Association of Collegiate Schools of Planning, Madison, WI, 1992.

Introductory information on careers and education in urban and regional planning, followed by profiles of master's programs in the U.S. and Canada. Includes an alphabetical list of faculty.

The Harvard College Premedical Guide. G. Sarah Gelberman. Office of Career Services, Faculty of Arts and Sciences, Harvard University, Cambridge, MA, 1993.

Discusses medicine as a career, the premedical curriculum and requirements, the application process, preparing for the interview, acceptance procedures, and financing medical education. Includes chapters on women and minorities in medicine, M.D.-Ph.D. programs, and postbaccalaureate premedical programs. Bibliography.

The Independent Study Catalog. National University Continuing Education Association, Peterson's, Princeton, NJ, triennial.

Alphabetical listing of institutions offering correspondence courses at the elementary, high school, vocational, college, and graduate levels, both credit and noncredit. Geographical index of external degree and certificate programs; subject index.

Inside the Law Schools: A Guide for Students by Students, 6th ed. S. F. Goldfarb. Plume, New York, NY, 1993.

Profiles of law schools based on reports from students and recent graduates. Includes information on placement and on accessibility for disabled students.

Insider's Guide to Graduate Programs in Clinical Psychology, 1994/1995 ed. Tracy J. Mayne, John C. Norcross, and Michael A. Sayette. The Guilford Press, New York, NY, annual.

Describes the field of clinical psychology; discusses choice of program and the application process, including the interview. Profiles the 175 APA-accredited clinical psychology programs in the U.S. and Canada. Appendixes include a time line, worksheets, research areas, and specialty clinics/practicum sites. Bibliography.

The Insider's Guide to the Top Ten Business Schools, 5th ed. Tom Fischgrund, editor. Little, Brown and Co., Boston, MA, 1993.

Profiles programs on the basis of curriculum, admissions, academic environment, social life, and placement. Includes a general section on getting into, succeeding in, and doing well after business school. Comparison chart of the programs.

Medical School Admission Requirements, United States and Canada. Association of American Medical Colleges, Washington, DC, annual.

Includes application information for medical schools in the United States and Canada, with introductory information on premedical planning and financial aid.

The Official Guide to MBA Programs. Graduate Management Admissions Council, Princeton, NJ, biennial.

Includes chapters on choosing a school, financing an MBA, etc. Presents tabular data, as well as in-depth profiles of schools worldwide.

The Official Guide to U.S. Law Schools. Law Schools Admission Services, Inc., Bantam Doubleday Dell, New York, NY, annual.

Presents an overview of the legal profession, discusses the law school application process, and profiles ABA-approved law schools. Includes financial aid information.

Peterson's Annual Guides to Graduate Study. Peterson's, Princeton, NJ, annual. 6 volumes.

Brief descriptions of accredited advanced degree programs in the U.S. and those in Canada, Mexico, Europe, and Africa that are accredited by U.S. accrediting bodies. Includes application, financial aid, and program size information. Contact names and phone numbers are included; full-page descriptions of some programs. Also available in CD-ROM format and online through DIALOG Information Services, Inc. (file 273).

Veterinary Medical School Admission Requirements in the United States and Canada. Association of American Veterinary Medical Colleges. Betz Publishing Co., Inc., Rockville, MD, annual.

Includes application and enrollment data, information on combined degree and other special programs, and financial aid information.

Financial Aid and Grants

Annual Register of Grant Support: A Directory of Funding Sources. R.R. Bowker, New Providence, NJ, annual.

Nonrepayable financial support programs, arranged by subject, with separate sections for international studies and special applicant populations (Black, Native American, Spanish-speaking, women). Eligibility and application information. Subject, organization/program, geographical, and personnel indexes.

Foundation Annual Reports.

Many foundations issue publicly obtainable annual reports. These reports account for the history, purpose, function, and current activities of the foundation, and can provide valuable information for the grant seeker. Each issue of *The Foundation Grants Index Quarterly*, published by the Foundation Center, New York, NY, contains a list of publications, including annual reports, available from grantmakers.

The Foundation Directory. The Foundation Center, New York, NY, annual.

Provides information on the nation's largest foundations. The subject and type of support (for example, "grants to individuals") indexes are quite useful. Identifies publicly accessible reference collections throughout the U.S. and describes Foundation Center publications and services in great detail.

Foundation Grants to Individuals, 9th ed. Carlotta R. Mills, editor. The Foundation Center, New York, NY, 1995.

Lists foundation grant programs for individuals (as opposed to those aimed at institutional support); includes a section on grants to individuals from countries other than the U.S. Foundation, subject, types of support, geographic focus, company employee grant, and specific educational institution indexes.

Free Money for People in the Arts. Laurie Blum. Collier Books, New York, NY, 1991.

Five sections: direct grants to individuals by subject; geographically restricted funding to individuals by state; fiscal sponsorship monies by state; federal funding sources; sample proposals. Subject index.

Grants and Awards Available to American Writers, 18th ed., 1994-95. PEN American Center, New York, NY, 1994.

Lists grants and awards available to American writers for use in the U.S. and abroad. Includes a section for grants and awards available to Canadian writers and a list of state arts councils. Awards, organizations, and categories indexes.

The Grants Register. Lisa Williams, editor. St. Martin's Press, New York, NY, biennial.

Intended primarily for students at or above the graduate level, the register lists scholarships, fellowships, research grants, exchange opportunities, competitions, prizes, and special awards. Includes eligibility and application information.

The Harvard College Guide to Grants. Lisa M. Muto & Paul A. Bohlmann. Office of Career Services, Faculty of Arts and Sciences, Harvard University, Cambridge, MA, 1994.

Basic information on fellowships and the application process. Includes grants for study in the U.S. and overseas, as well as grants for work and practical experience. Annotated bibliography. Cross-indexes: grants for minorities and women; grants for freshmen, sophomores, and juniors; grants for summer and short-term projects; and grants for professional graduate study. Alphabetical index of grants.

The Official Guide to Financing Your MBA. Graduate Management Admission Council, Princeton, NJ, biennial.

Includes chapters on financial planning, debt management, international students, etc. Glossary.

Peterson's Grants for Graduate & Post-Doctoral Study, 4th ed. Peterson's, Princeton, NJ, 1995.

Introductory information on the grant-seeking process, followed by an alphabetical listing of grant and fellowship programs. Includes contact, eligibility, and application information. Subject and special characteristics (e.g., citizenship, ethnic minority, gender, etc.) indexes.

Scholarships, Fellowships and Loans: A Guide to Education-Related Financial Aid Programs for Students and Professionals. Debra M. Kirby, editor. Gale Research Inc., Detroit, MI, biennial.

Includes information on eligibility requirements, selection criteria, application deadlines, and contact information. Vocational goals, field of study, legal resident, place of study, special recipient, and sponsor/scholarship indexes.

State Foundation Directories.

Directories of private foundations registered with the state as charitable, tax-exempt institutions are available for most states. These are helpful in identifying smaller foundations not listed in other sources like *The Foundation Directory*.

Chapter 4

JOB SEARCH

INTRODUCTION

In your ongoing search for career development opportunities, you will be on the lookout for challenging work that you might want to undertake. The search for opportunities to develop your skills, gain knowledge and experience, and contribute to an endeavor that you consider worthwhile continues even when you are fully employed. In evaluating work opportunities, you will want to give priority to what you can learn and what you can accomplish. Do not limit your search to regular full-time jobs. A project done on contract might be an opportunity to build your professional reputation. Or, you may identify an opportunity to start your own business.

As a career entrepreneur, you should seek information about new trends, markets, and technologies. You may learn about potential opportunities from a news item on television or in the newspaper, a neighbor or a friend, a professional journal, or an on-line bulletin board. You are not looking for a job listing—you are looking for ideas about work that needs to be done. Once a job is described and advertised, there are lots of candidates waiting in line. Your goal is to find an executive who needs something done and convince him that, either as his employee or on contract, you can fulfill his need. Or, your goal is to discover a niche in the market for a product or service and to start your own business.

You are very likely to hear about opportunities through your professional or personal network. When an employer has a job to fill or when he has an unmet need, he usually talks to his friends about it before listing it, because he prefers to hire someone referred by a colleague. The first group that he is likely to communicate with is his professional network—his colleagues in the same industry—but he is quite likely to also mention his needs to his friends. Members of his network will spread news of the opportunity to members of their networks and soon you may hear about the job opportunity from someone you'know.

The functions of a job search that are described in this chapter are not sequential steps, but interdependent, ongoing activities that you engage in as you pursue work possibilities. For each type of work that you pursue, you must research the employers and the industry or field. As you identify employers for whom you would like to do work, you will want to make contact with them to learn about their organization and to increase your visibility as a person interested in their work. The knowledge that you gain from your research will enable you to improve the appropriateness, clarity, and sophistication of your presentation for job openings.

As you move from one job to another, you will be in contact with hundreds of people, and will research many organizations. In your career research file, described in Chapter 2, you should keep a record of every contact you make and of the outcome of each contact; copies of every letter sent and received; notes on your interviews, not only about the content of the conversation, but also your reactions and observations; and notes on your research. This information should be organized and filed so that it is retrievable. Remember that you are engaged in a lifelong process. At any time, because of a change in your employment or a change of your priorities, you might decide to look for a new job. At that time, you might need to review the information in your job search files from a new perspective.

False Assumptions about Searching for Work

1. **Contacts can get you the job.** Wrong. Your network of friends and contacts in your career field is your most important resource in your job search. They are a source of information, support, and referrals. However, although their support may get you an interview for a job, only you can win yourself a job offer.

2. **You are imposing on an employer when you initiate contact with him to express interest in his organization.** Usually not. Executives are on the lookout for talent to meet their present or future needs. If you have expertise that an employer values, he will be interested in

meeting you, and if you impress him, you may become part of his talent pool.

3. **Employers can assess in an interview whether you are the person to do the job.** That depends on you. Employers do not have mystical powers that enable them to divine your suitability to meet their needs. You must communicate your qualifications. Even if the employers are experienced in assessing candidates, it is your responsibility to convey why you feel you are the best candidate to do the job.

4. **Employers will hire the person with the best job skills.** Not always. Employers look for personal qualities as well as job skills. They want a person whom they like and who will fit in with the other employees. Many skills can be learned on the job, but personal qualities are more difficult to develop or change. Different employers look for different qualities, but all employers balance the job skills and personal qualities of candidates when selecting new employees.

5. **All job openings are advertised.** Not true. It is estimated that only 10 to 20 percent of job openings are advertised publicly. Many jobs are filled by promoting people from within the organization. Other jobs are filled by the employer informing his colleagues that he has a job to fill. If, through your networking, you become known as being competent and effective, you may be the person the colleague recommends for his friend's job opening.

6. **It is better to take a job with an established company than to start your own business.** Not necessarily. That depends on your assessment of the business opportunity and your willingness to take risks. Managers are increasingly seeking outside contractors to provide services and products essential to their organizations.

RESEARCHING EMPLOYMENT OPPORTUNITIES

Researching employers is a continuing process which becomes more intensive when you are exploring a specific possibility. The more descriptive and evaluative information about potential employers and their organizations that you have, the better you will be able to determine your interest and to tailor your approach.

Employers assume that if you are interested in their organization, you will take time to learn something about it before your first contact. One reason it is wise to focus on one or two types of work is that it enables you to concentrate your research on that industry or field, the organizations within the field, and the job possibilities.

Information about Industries or Professions

To gain background on an industry or profession, you need to know about its history, impact on society, organizational structure, products and services, and expected growth. You are interested in information about current issues and developments, and the impact of economic and political trends.

Potentially interesting information is available all around you: on television; in newspapers, magazines, and books; and from online databases. And, as always, people can be the most valuable source of information. Keep your professional network and personal friends informed about the industries and employers that you are exploring so that they can help you gather information.

Career literature, similar in structure to the literature in an academic field, will be especially valuable. There are books that relate the history of organizations, describe the leaders, analyze the present financial status, and/or give predictions for the future. There are professional journals and newspapers that give news of current events, discuss issues, report research findings, and describe innovative programs. The section on Using Career Literature in Chapter 2 and the bibliography at the end of that chapter will introduce you to some of these publications.

You should review regularly the magazines, journals, and newspapers that your targeted employers read. Become informed on newsworthy developments relating to their field, and learn to understand them from their perspective.

Information about Corporations or Organizations

Before you make contact with a corporate employer, you should have basic information about the company: its reputation, products or services;

number of employees; location of plants and offices; sales, assets and earnings; growth pattern and new products or services. If it is an educational institution, you want to know about its history and traditions, current programs, financial status, and the demographics of the student body. If it is a government department, you need information about its place in the organizational structure, and its budget stability, mandate, and recent history. With every organization, you want as much information as you can gather about its recent history and future direction.

The corporate annual report or other company literature, the college or school catalogue, government manuals, and directories will contain this information. There are indexes to periodical literature for all major career fields. Looking up the name of a corporation in the *Business Periodicals Index* or *F&S Index United States* gives you a list of recent journal and newspaper articles about that corporation. The *Current Index to Journals in Education* is the best guide to recent articles about educational institutions. *The Readers Guide to Periodical Literature* or newspaper indexes such as the *Wall Street Journal Index* and the *New York Times Index* are helpful for many career fields. The *Gale Directory of Databases* will identify online and CD-ROM sources of information.

Information about Jobs and Work Environments

When you identify an interesting opportunity, you want to research how the work is accomplished, how responsibilities are described and assigned, and the style of supervision. It is also important to analyze the potential for increasing your expertise and making a contribution, and to evaluate the support for innovation and expansion of your responsibilities over time. You also want to learn about the people who work in the organization, their interpersonal relationships, and their morale and commitment. Finally, you want to learn about the human and physical characteristics of the work environment. Referring back to the Work Dimensions section in Chapter 2 may be helpful in identifying the questions that you want to be asking about each opportunity.

Only limited information about these human factors is available in print. Most of this information you will learn from your own observations and from people who are familiar with the organization. You can learn a great deal through interviews if you have planned in advance what you want to ask. When you are being considered for a specific position, you should ask to meet with the person who currently has the job or with someone in a similar position. You may also be able to identify people who used to work for the organization who can give you an inside/outside perspective.

Job hunters sometimes fail to think analytically about their personal observations. When you are visiting a potential employer, you have the opportunity to observe many characteristics of the work environment: the style of the manager, the physical surroundings, the people, the interpersonal relationships, the pace of the work. When you are recording the information which you gained in your interviews, include your impressions and reactions to being in the work setting. In thinking about the question "Would I be happy in this organization?" give careful attention to the subjective data from your personal observations during your visit.

Information about Opportunities to Create Your Own Employment

If your objective is to find an opportunity to create your own business, you will utilize the same extensive array of resources, but your focus will be on identifying unmet needs or inefficiencies. There are increasing opportunities for the small entrepreneur today to provide a service or a product of improved quality for less cost. The services that employers find it economical to contract out are often functions such as generating monthly paychecks, producing fund-raising mailings, or searching for new employees. A product that you might produce and sell at a profit could be anything that would help other organizations operate more efficiently.

PRESENTING YOURSELF

When applying for a job or following up on a referral, you must communicate to the employer that you have the qualities that he is seeking. By means of your resume and attachments, cover letter, and letters of reference (if you decide to send them), you want to communicate to the employer that you are the kind of person who will be a productive and respected worker in his organization.

Clarifying What You Have to Offer

Often liberal arts graduates and graduate students think employers are looking for specific job-related skills. To some extent and for certain types of jobs, this is true. Job listings often indicate a requirement of two to five years of directly related experience. In reality, however, employers are often looking for somebody they will enjoy, who will fit into their organization, and who can readily learn to do the job that needs to be done.

The following questions will help you identify work characteristics that you have which employers value.

Do you set high standards for yourself and persevere to achieve your goals? Any evidence of high achievement, such as academic honors, varsity athletics, or awards in music or the arts, is a sign that you set high standards and have the discipline to endure long periods of training and practice for delayed gratification. To show that you are goal-oriented, speak in terms of achievements rather than in terms of effort expended or functions performed.

Are you sensitive to others' feelings and cheerful and thoughtful in your interaction with colleagues? Almost all work requires that you relate to other people. Employers look for people whom they enjoy and who will be compatible with colleagues and clients.

Do you have a high level of energy and are you able to channel it into productive efforts? People who lead busy lives, engaging in a variety of activities, yet meeting their responsibilities and deadlines, are people with high energy levels and self-discipline.

Are you cooperative? Do you take instruction well and work well with others? Are you flexible about what tasks you do and how you do them? Experience in working with others on projects and programs or in team sports teaches you to be an effective team member.

Are you innovative? Do you think creatively about procedures and objectives? Do you enjoy looking at situations in new ways?

Do you have the ability to lead, organize, and supervise other people? Leadership experience in any kind of organization provides you with the opportunity to develop these skills. Be sure your resume describes the leadership experiences you have had.

Do you take initiative? Do you wait to be instructed before you act or do you act on your own, thinking through new ways to get the job done?

Have you had the experience of losing as well as winning? Are you able to lose and continue to give your best effort? Experience in winning and losing comes most dramatically in athletics, but there are many types of competitive activities in which you may have won and lost.

Do you view change as a positive challenge? Do you seek new adventures? Are you enthusiastic about learning new skills and applying new knowledge? Are you excited about assuming new responsibilities? Do you see change as an opportunity to be creative?

Are you a risk-taker? Are you energized by a high-risk environment or are you more productive in a low-risk environment? How do you deal with uncertainty? Do you move forward and become more productive or do you prefer to wait for clarification? What experience do you have in adapting to new situations?

Do you have the capacity to be loyal? Are you loyal to your friends, your college, former employers, your family, your hometown? It is not the object of your loyalty but your capacity for loyalty that will interest employers. If you are negative and critical about your past jobs and associations, employers will be concerned you might be that way about their organization.

Do you get along well with people who are different from you in race, ethnicity, gender, and sexual orientation? Do you have experience living and working with a diverse group of individuals?

Do you have high expectations of yourself? Do you have high aspirations? Employers ask what you hope to be doing in five or ten years to get an indication of how ambitious you are.

These are all qualities which may be important to an employer as he evaluates candidates for a specific position in his organization. You have probably developed some of these attributes more than others. In your job search, you should be prepared to communicate the work qualities and competencies that you have developed by describing past achievements in both your written materials and interviews.

As a liberal arts student or graduate student you have highly developed analytic, research, and communication skills. In the university, where your colleagues are articulate, learn quickly, and reason clearly, you may take these skills for granted, but to an employer they may be your most important qualifications. Remember that the employer values the person who is bright, thoughtful, and decisive, and able to express himself well in writing or in speech.

You may already have some specific work skills which make you attractive to an employer. The following are a few of the skills which it is possible to acquire through academic courses:

- accounting
- bibliographic research
- computer applications
- computer programming
- filmmaking
- foreign language fluency
- laboratory research
- math and statistics
- writing

If you are interested in work that requires specific skills that you can learn in academic courses, it is wise to take these courses as electives, or as evening, summer school, or correspondence courses. For a list of resources see the Graduate and Professional Education section of the bibliography at the end of Chapter 3. Some students prefer to learn subjects such as math, statistics, computer programming, or accounting on their own. Books in the Schaum's Outline Series which are listed in the bibliography at the end of this chapter are programmed texts for self-study which you can use to learn these skills. Check the shelves of your local library, bookstore, or computer software store for similar self-study materials.

It may be that your field of study either as an undergraduate or as a graduate student will be relevant in your job hunt. For example, specific knowledge in the sciences, applied math, economics, foreign languages, or regional studies can be relevant to certain jobs in business and government. However, the purpose of this section has been to alert you to the general work qualifications which you have been developing during your formal education that are important to employers.

Communicating Your Strengths to Employers

You need to be able to talk about yourself: to describe how you approach work, what kind of tasks you do best, what types of goals you set for yourself, what sorts of interpersonal relationships you handle effectively, and what kinds of roles you usually take in an organization. The way you describe your past experiences and achievements will communicate to employers the kind of worker you would be in their organization.

Every career field has its own vocabulary which you will be learning from your reading and information interviews. In planning your resume and cover letter, and preparing for your job interview, you should use the employer's vocabulary to describe your past experiences and work attributes.

USING JOB LISTINGS

Because only 10-20 percent of jobs get publicly listed, you do not want to limit your search to applying for listed jobs. However, job listings are one source of information about how work is being structured and what work needs to be done. It is certainly worthwhile to identify the best source for job listings in your field and geographic area. Even if you do not find any jobs listed for which you wish to apply, the descriptions may generate ideas of the kinds of work that you would like or identify potential employers or entrepreneurial opportunities.

On-Campus Recruiting

Most schools have placement or career planning offices which provide a variety of resources: job listings sent in by employers seeking recent graduates, newsletters with a sampling of the job listings, a career forum or fair, an on-campus recruiting program, and a career reference library.

On-campus recruiting provides the opportunity to interview for certain types of jobs at your college or university, but keep in mind that only certain types of industries recruit on campus, and in those industries only a small number of employers schedule campus visits. For jobs in other industries, you have to take the initiative to research potential employers and contact them.

If you participate in on-campus recruiting, you should make your choices with care. If you are not interested in a company, do not waste your time and that of the recruiter by signing up just for the interviewing experience. This will not benefit you, it will annoy the recruiter, and it will deprive a classmate of a valuable opportunity.

You should prepare for your on-campus interview by carefully researching the organization and career field for which you are being considered. After the interview, you should promptly send a thank-you note to your interviewer. This will help you distinguish yourself from the many students who were interviewed at the same time.

Even for the industries that are represented in recruiting, you should not rely solely on on-campus recruiting for a job after graduation. On-campus recruiters represent only a small sample of the employers who might be interested in hiring you. In addition, you may be more successful in securing an interview when you contact an organization on your own; your letter and resume may receive a closer reading than if they were part of a large shipment!

Newspaper Want Ads

The largest collection of local help wanted ads is usually found in the Sunday edition of a city newspaper such as the *Boston Globe* or the *Los Angeles Times*. You will find three kinds of want ads: those placed by employment agencies, listing the types of jobs that they have available; large want ads from large corporations; and very small want ads from small employers.

Want ads in local or suburban papers are sometimes the best way to learn about jobs in small organizations. It is less expensive to advertise in the local papers, and sometimes small employers prefer to reach only the audience to which the local paper is distributed. If you do a comprehensive review of newspaper want ad sections and job listings as you begin your job hunt, you can assess which papers you want to continue to review regularly.

Institutional Job Listings

Most universities, hospitals, and other large institutions publish job listings on a regular basis. Large employers have a human resources department and that is usually the place where jobs are posted. If you are hoping to find a job with a particular employer, it is usually worthwhile to visit the human resources department to see what their recruitment process is and to make personal contact with someone in that office.

Where to Find Job Listings in Your Career Field

Most career fields have trade and professional journals or newspapers in which there are job listings. For example, social service and community organization jobs are listed in the monthly newspaper *Community Jobs*; jobs in the performing arts are listed in *ArtSEARCH*, published twenty-three times a year; and *International Employment Opportunities* lists current openings in the U.S. and abroad in all sectors of the job market.

The *Standard Periodical Directory* can lead you to job listings; it has an Employment section that lists, by career field, all the periodicals that regularly publish job listings, such as the three cited above.

The Internet can also be a good place to locate job listings, especially through Usenet newsgroups and the many gophers from around the world. Some organizations even put information about themselves and opportunities with them on the World Wide Web. Because new listings appear daily, it is important to surf the Internet frequently when you are in job-search mode.

Employment Agencies

Most employment agencies specialize in a particular segment of the job market. By reading the want ads, you can identify employment agencies which list jobs in your career field. The first thing to ascertain about an employment agency is who is paying for the service. If you are paying for the service, the agency will expect a generous percentage of your first-year income if you take a job listed through them. If the employer is paying for the service, there should be no charge to you.

State employment offices will serve you without charge, and many list professional jobs. If you decide to use a state employment service, try to identify a counselor who seems interested in you and make contact with that person every week.

Executive search firms are paid by employers to recruit executives for their company. They are not in business to assist graduates in finding first jobs. Usually they are looking for highly skilled, experienced professionals who might be willing to consider a new position.

Answering Want Ads: Applying for Jobs

In applying for a job, always write a cover letter to send with your resume. Take a day to research the position that is listed and to learn about how the search is being conducted. Try to get information about the employer and the job. If it is a large company, you can obtain a copy of an annual report and other information as you would for an on-campus recruiter. If it is a small employer, you may have to rely on talking with people who know the organization. If your career exploration has been focusing on that type of work, you probably already know some people who can give you information about the employer.

Many want ads request that the applicant have three to five years of experience. If you do not have any full-time work experience in the field, you may still apply, but you must describe how your paid and unpaid experiences have prepared you for this job.

Since listed jobs represent only a small portion of the job market, you should check listings at regular intervals, but your greatest investment of time and energy should be spent in initiating contact with potential employers.

IDENTIFYING AND CONTACTING POTENTIAL EMPLOYERS

Taking the initiative to meet employers for whom you would like to work is a very important part of managing your career. Your objective in asking to meet with these employers is to learn about their career experiences and their company. From the beginning, make it clear that you are seeking information and advice, not asking for a job. Express your interest in learning about their career experiences. Most people enjoy talking about themselves and you can gain valuable insights from their stories. You will make a favorable impression if you listen enthusiastically and ask perceptive questions.

Your agenda is also to make personal contact with people who have the power to hire you and to use the opportunity to present your interest in and qualifications for working in their organization. If the interview goes well and the employer is impressed with your potential, he may recommend that you contact some of his colleagues in the same or other organizations.

If each employer that you interview refers you to at least one other potential employer, you will quickly expand your network of people in your career field who know your qualifications and interests. Although initially you may want to meet with young employees to learn about the organization, eventually you want to have the opportunity to meet and interview with top executives. It is generally high-level executives who have the overview, insight, and power to think creatively about how a talented candidate might be useful in their organization.

If you have a Ph.D. and are job hunting on the nonacademic job market, it is important that you research companies and assess your own skills and values to find good matches before you contact potential employers. *Outside the Ivory Tower: A Guide for Academics Considering Alternative Careers* will be a helpful reference if you are undertaking this process. When you are ready to contact employers, you will want to meet with high-level executives in order to discuss with them what you could bring to their organization.

Identifying Potential Employers

From your study of job listings in your career field, you may have several kinds of helpful information. If you have learned about the types of jobs for which you have applied, you may next try to identify other employers who might have similar jobs. If an employer is advertising jobs that are too advanced for you, you might contact that employer anyway, because he might promote someone from within and then have a lower-level job opening for which you are qualified. If your preferred employer is not listing jobs in any resource that you have studied, do not despair; for a variety of reasons some employers do not list jobs publicly.

Again, people are the best source of names of potential employers. The members of your network will be interested in hearing what you are learning from your research and other members of your network and how your goals are evolving. Not all of your contacts with people in your network need to be in person. You might sometimes talk on the telephone or perhaps communicate by e-mail or letter. By whatever method of communication they prefer, give them an update on your progress and ask if they can suggest other people you should be meeting.

To add to your personal contacts in your chosen career field, you should talk to everyone about your job objectives: your academic adviser, tutor, former employers, friends, friends' parents, family, and neighbors. A personal referral increases the likelihood that you will get an interview with a potential employer. Once in the interview, however, you are on your own. You will be hired only if you convince the employer that you are the best person for the job.

Every career field has directories which list organizations and give information about them. From a directory you can learn the names of executives of the organization, addresses, and other information. For large companies, you should write to the manager of the division in which you would like to work. For a middle-size company, you should write to the chief executive officer.

In the professional journals of your chosen field, you can learn about potential employers: persons who are mentioned in news articles or interviewed by journals or who write articles published in the journals. When contacting somebody about whom you have read, you should always tell him where you learned his name.

If you are conducting a long-distance job search or have a specific geographic destination, useful sources are directories which have geographic indexes and job bulletins on the Internet. There are usually local and state employer directories available and every community has classifieds. A little research will tell you which local newspaper has the best want ads and where you can find that newspaper. The local alumni club may have lists of alumni career advisers in the area. This may be your most valuable resource for initiating your network in your new community.

Contacting Potential Employers

It is important that your materials and style of making contact be appropriate to the industry. It is wise to ask someone in your network to review drafts of your resume and cover letters so that he can help you refine your presentation. The best guideline to how aggressive, assertive, and persistent you should be is your judgment of how much those qualities are valued in the job and the field to which you are applying.

The usual way of making contact with a potential employer is by writing a letter expressing your interest in his organization and career field. You will usually enclose a resume, but you may include information about your educational and employment background in the letter if you prefer. In some career fields, making initial contact by telephone is acceptable and may be more productive. When someone gives you a referral, you might ask how you should make the contact. Also seek guidance in job-hunting strategy and style from your career advisers.

You may want to consider submitting your resume to an electronic resume database which employers can access to identify potential employees. If an employer uses a resume database system, the search is done by job-related skills. Therefore, resume database services may be appropriate for candidates with job-related academic degrees or specific work competencies such as engineering, computer science, science, and foreign languages. What these databases do not communicate is the candidate's personal qualities and important skills such as analytical thinking and writing and speaking ability.

Resume databases are businesses which are paid for by either the candidate or the employer. If you are considering submitting your resume, be sure that you evaluate the service with questions such as the following:

- What employers are using the database and how often?
- Does the service provide the employer with a summary of information about the candidate, or the complete, original resume?
- Will the service offer you suggestions on how to revise your resume to improve your computer match rate?
- How long will your resume remain on the system?

Evidence that resume databases are productive for the job seeker is not readily available. However, the fact that many commercial attempts to develop a national resume database system have failed would seem to indicate that employers are not using them extensively to identify and recruit new employees.

The Employer's Perspective

- Employers are interested in young people who have chosen their career field. Most mid-career people enjoy being helpful and giving advice to those who are looking for opportunities in their field.

- Employers will usually consent to interviews with people who have been referred by friends or colleagues. If the friend is someone whom they respect, they will agree to the interview with the expectation that you are somebody who will be of interest to them.

- Employers look for talent. Most employers, even if they do not have any open jobs at the moment, are interested in identifying people who might be productive members of their organization in the future.

DESIGNING YOUR JOB

There is a great range of possibilities for structuring how, where, when, and by whom work is accomplished. It is important for you to think about the range of alternatives as you plan your next move so that you are prepared to explore your preferred options with potential employers. If a specific option such as being able to work at home becomes a strong priority or a requirement for you, then the feasibility of that option should be explored early in researching any opportunity. However, if being able to work at home is desirable but not necessary, you might explore that option after you have a job offer or you have been on the job for a while.

"HOW work gets done" is changing all the time with the rapid acceptance of new technology for production and for communication. Focusing on quality of output, organizations are streamlining their processes of production. All members of organizations are asked to think about how they can improve their efficiency and quality of output. Teamwork is usually required to redesign work, but any individual may take the initiative in suggesting innovations. The ease of distributing information within and between organizations has changed how and by whom decisions are made.

"WHERE work gets done" is changing. It used to be that most types of employees had to be in the office to get work done because of the equipment that they used, information they needed to access, and interaction with fellow workers that the work required. Now, with computers, many workers can work anywhere that they have computer, modem, and fax. Increasing numbers of workers are telecommuting—working at home or at an office near home and saving the time and expense of commuting.

"WHEN work gets done" can sometimes be varied. If the work requires interaction of the team or availability to customers, this must be given priority, but it does not necessarily require that all staff members work exactly the same hours. Some employers allow flex-time so that workers can adjust their work schedule to accommodate their family schedule or to decrease their commuting time.

"BY WHOM work gets done" questions the assumption that to meet an identified need, the manager must add an employee to his workforce. Employers are discovering that it is sometimes more efficient to hire a temporary worker or to contract out the work. When there is an uneven demand for a particular function, such as sending out a large mailing, employers often hire temporary workers to get the task done. If the task is one that occurs periodically, such as end-of-the-month financial transactions, the manager may contract with a business services firm. If the task is specialized, such as writing the annual report, the manager might hire a freelance writer. If you would prefer to have the freedom and flexibility of working on contract or as a freelancer, *Workstyles to Fit Your Lifestyle: Everyone's Guide to Temporary Employment*, listed in the Self-Assessment section of the bibliography at the end of Chapter 3, might be a helpful reference.

The timing and process of designing your job varies extensively with how strongly you feel about the alternatives, how much of a risk-taker you are, and what expertise you have. It is, of course, often possible to arrange more flexibility in where and when you do your work with an employer who knows you and with whom you have a strong work history. Going out on your own offers the possibility of control over all the alternatives above, but in reality, you may discover that it takes constant marketing and acceptance of all work offered in order to support yourself. If you want to be your own boss or work freelance someday, you should select work experiences now that will allow you to develop skills and expertise for which there is high demand.

How much flexibility you have in how, where, when, and for whom you work is up to you. If you are interested in alternatives to a nine-to-five job in an office setting, you should consult widely with members of your network about how to make this happen. You might also want to consult books like *GoodWorks: A Guide to Careers in Social Change* or *Jobs in Paradise: The Definitive Guide to Exotic Jobs Everywhere*, listed in the bibliography at the end of Chapter 2.

CREATING YOUR OWN EMPLOYMENT

You may decide to become self-employed and work free-lance or as a consultant or to develop your own business because that is what you have always wanted to do, or because that is the way you can get paid for doing the work you most want to be doing. Your self-employment may be lifelong or only temporary between other types of employment. Sometimes working on contract or as a consultant offers the best opportunity for developing expertise and accomplishing something.

If you want to be self-employed, you will need to develop a service or product for which someone wants to pay you. There are a great variety of possibilities, from writing and editing to research and information services to tutoring and teaching.

If you want to develop a business, you will need to develop a business plan which includes a description of your product, the market you anticipate, the production process, and the sources and amount of start-up capital needed. The directories and indexes listed in the bibliography at the end of this chapter can help you in your research.

To promote your services, you will need an attractively packaged portfolio which includes a resume, samples of your work, and references. To reach new markets, seek the advice and support of your network. Talk to everyone who might be able to help you build your business. Identify appropriate places to advertise your services, and send your portfolio to every prospect that you identify.

CONSIDERING TEMPORARY WORK

Temporary employment agencies are an important option to consider during an interim between jobs or during a time when you want more control over when and how much you work. Temporary assignments are no longer limited to secretarial jobs, but now include many types of professional assignments as well. The positive aspects of temp work are that it provides an opportunity to

- earn income
- build skills and learn new skills
- expand your work experience
- receive regular performance reviews
- try out a variety of work environments
- get a sense of a company and the people who work there
- become, perhaps, an inside candidate for a permanent position
- have flexibility—you decide whether you want to work full-time, part-time, evenings, weekends, and for what term

Some negative aspects include:

- not all assignments are interesting; some are boring
- most temp assignments are full-time which may make it difficult to continue an aggressive job search
- you may feel like an outsider
- health and retirement benefits are ordinarily not available

When you are a temp worker, your "employer" is the temporary employment agency and the "client" is the company hiring your services through the agency. The agency will offer you assignments based on your skills and interests. Your rate of pay is determined by your skills, experience, and performance evaluation. You will receive your paycheck from the agency. Under certain circumstances, you may qualify for paid vacation time and health and life insurance benefits through the agency.

Selecting Temporary Employment Agencies

- Check the classifieds; the heading is usually Employment Contractors-Temporary Help.

- Ask each agency what types of employers and what jobs they have.
- Ask what free training programs they offer to help you increase your skills.
- Ask what benefits they offer.
- If there is a specific business or organization where you would like to work, call the human resources department and ask what agency they use when they need temporary help.

Applying at Temp Agencies

Most agencies prefer that you telephone first and set up an appointment for an interview. You will be required to complete an extensive application about your work history and skills, such as word processing and other computer skills, accounting, and languages, and to list two work references. It may be relevant to describe your part-time jobs and volunteer experience. You can save time if you bring a copy of your resume. In addition, you will probably be asked to take a typing or word processing test to determine your speed and accuracy, and you will be interviewed to assess your interpersonal skills, work style, and preferences.

You may want to discuss the following topics with the agency representative:

- typical work assignments and hourly rate for a person with your skills
- examples of employers with whom they do the most business
- the average length of assignments
- the possibility of evening or part-time assignments
- the availability of benefits, especially health
- the paycheck schedule

You should apply to several temporary employment agencies. Different agencies have different jobs. Employers tend to develop relationships with a specific agency or agencies. If there are particular types of employers where you would like to work, it is best to shop for an agency that does a lot of business with that type of employer.

Tips about Temping

You've been hired to get work done. Be on time! Ask the supervisor for instruction on what to do and how to do it, if you need it, and then get to work. If you finish your assigned work, ask the supervisor if you can be of assistance on other projects. Your performance on your first assignment is very important; you are establishing your reputation with the agency.

Many corporations hire through temporary agencies. Rather than listing their jobs, they engage temp workers to try them out. They then make offers of permanent employment to those who impress them with their work habits and their ability to fit into their environment.

CONTINUE YOUR JOB SEARCH! One way is to select temp work that allows you to build your job skills and/or make contacts in your field of interest. If this is not possible, look for opportunities to volunteer in your chosen field.

SURVIVING THE JOB HUNT

Job hunting takes time and energy. During most of your lifetime you will be developing work opportunities while you are employed or self-employed, since gathering information and looking for ideas of work that needs to be done will be an ongoing activity. The key to being successful at this entrepreneurial approach to your career development is good time management.

If you are job hunting full-time, you should plan your schedule as seriously as if you were being paid to conduct this search. Set objectives for the number of employers you will write to and the number of interviews you will schedule each week. Develop a daily routine: for example, interviews in the morning, lunch with friends, library research in the afternoon, letter writing or reading in the evening, or whatever makes sense for you. But make a schedule and keep to it.

If you are job hunting while you are still a college or graduate student, set aside a half-day or more each week to devote to your search. If you are job hunting while you are a temporary worker, you may want to ask for part-time assignments or arrange for a few days off between assignments. If you are employed, you can do your research and letter writing in the evenings and on weekends, but you will probably have to arrange to take time off for interviews.

Be clear about your goals. The best opportunity to develop expertise and add to your professional reputation might be a project job on contract or a consulting assignment. As employers increase their reliance on contract workers, there are significant entrepreneurial opportunities in developing businesses that provide services to organizations on contract.

If you are unemployed, be realistic about your financial needs. If you do not have savings to support yourself for several months, you will probably want to find a temporary part-time job so that you have some income coming in.

Most job markets are very competitive. With each job you apply for, there will be many candidates and you are much more likely to be rejected than to be selected. Although it takes a great deal of energy, it is always best to be pursuing several jobs simultaneously. Even when you are a final candidate for a job, you should continue applying for new jobs. Maybe you will generate several job offers at once and can choose the one that suits you best.

Job hunting can be discouraging. It is hard to keep up your morale when you are not getting positive responses to your letters or interviews. Job hunters need friends to share their ups and downs. Find someone who is willing to listen as you relate your experiences or join a local job hunter networking group. Talking about your interviews and observations can help you assess these experiences and revise your plans accordingly. Checking in with your career counselor at regular intervals also provides an opportunity for you to review your progress and think together about the next step.

If you have been job hunting full-time for two or three months and have not had an offer, you may want to broaden either your job objective or your geographic area. You do not need to stop applying for your first-choice type of job, but broadening your objectives may result in an earlier job offer.

Another option to consider is volunteer work. Being a volunteer can give you relevant experience, bolster your self-confidence, and provide the opportunity to work with people in your chosen field. It may also lead to paid employment.

Undertaking an aggressive job hunt increases the likelihood of getting the job you want. Getting the job that launches your career by being in the right place at the right time and knowing the right people may appear to be the result of chance, but it is more often the end result of carefully planned career research, networking, and job searching.

SOURCES

Directories

General

College Placement Council Directory. College Placement Council, Bethlehem, PA, annual.
> Lists recruiting personnel at colleges and college relations/human resources recruitment personnel at corporate/government/service organizations. Geographic index of employers. Lists special interest networks (engineering, liberal arts, MBA); includes information on the College Placement Council.

The Directory of Executive Recruiters. Kennedy Publications, Fitzwilliam, NH, annual.
> Introductory information for candidates and clients, followed by separate sections for retainer firms and contingency firms. Function, industry, geographic, key principals, and firm indexes; annotated bibliography.

Job Choices Series. College Placement Council, Inc., Bethlehem, PA, annual. 4 volumes.
> Volume 1 offers general advice on careers and job hunting. Volume 2 profiles employers seeking candidates for business and administrative positions. Volume 3 does the same for technical positions. Volume 4 provides information on employers seeking graduates in health care fields.

Minority Organizations: A National Directory, 4th ed. Garrett Park Press, Garrett Park, MD, 1992.
> Alphabetical listing of groups established by or serving American Indians, Native Alaskans, Blacks, Hispanics, and Asian Americans. Geographic, program/service area, and membership organization indexes. Bibliography.

Places Rated Almanac: Your Guide to Finding the Best Places to Live in North America. David Savageau and Richard Boyer. Prentice Hall Travel, New York, NY, 1993.
> Describes and ranks U.S. metropolitan areas on various factors, including cost of living, jobs, housing, crime, recreation, etc. A good place to begin when contemplating a change of scenery.

Research Centers Directory. Anthony L. Gerring, editor. Gale Research Inc., Detroit, MI, annual. 2 volumes.
> Subject listing of university-related and nonprofit research organizations in the U.S. and Canada; gives research activities and fields, as well as

publications, services, and staff size. Subject, geographic, personal name, and alphabetic indexes. Updated by New Research Centers. Also available online through DIALOG.

Arts and Media

Artist's & Graphic Designer's Market: Where & How to Sell Your Illustration, Fine Art, Graphic Design, & Cartoons. Mary Cox, editor. Writer's Digest Books, Cincinnati, OH, annual.

Introductory chapters on "The Business of Art," followed by a classified listing of the markets, from advertising to syndicates. Includes interviews with individuals with successful art careers. Lists artists' reps, organizations, and publications of interest. Glossary. Humor and general indexes.

Billboard International Buyer's Guide. BPI Communications, New York, NY, annual.

Record companies, video studios, music publishers, services, organizations, etc., for the music industry. Includes some international listings.

Editor and Publisher International Yearbook. Editor & Publisher, New York, NY, annual.

Geographic listings of: daily, weekly, and specialized newspapers in the U.S. and Canada; general interest newspapers in the rest of the world. Includes information on services, organizations, education, foreign correspondents in the U.S., etc. Also available in CD-ROM format.

Handel's National Directory for the Performing Arts, 5th ed. R.R. Bowker, New Providence, NJ, 1992. 2 volumes.

Volume 1 lists organizations and facilities geographically, and is indexed by arts area (dance, instrumental music, vocal music, theater, performing series, facility). Volume 2 lists educational institutions geographically, with dance, music, and theater indexes. Each volume also has a general index.

Hollywood Creative Directory. Santa Monica, CA, three times yearly.

Alphabetically lists motion picture and TV development and production companies and staff; cross-references companies with studio deals; company type and name indexes.

The International Directory of Little Magazines and Small Presses. Len Fulton, editor. Dustbooks, Paradise, CA, annual.

Alphabetical listing, with regional and subject indexes.

International Motion Picture Almanac. Quigley Publishing Co., Inc., New York, NY, annual.

Arranged by service, activity, or other category, with facts and figures. Includes a section entitled "Who's Who in Motion Pictures and Television." Subject index.

International Television and Video Almanac. Quigley Publishing Co., Inc., New York, NY, annual.
Arranged by service, activity, or other category, with facts and figures. Includes a "Who's Who" section. Subject index.

Literary Agents: A Writer's Guide. Adam Begley. Penguin Books, New York, NY, 1993.
Chapters on finding an agent, the author-agent relationship, the writing business, etc. Lists agents and resources.

Literary Market Place: The Directory of the American Book Publishing Industry with Industry Yellow Pages. R.R. Bowker Co., New Providence, NJ, annual.
Lists publishers, organizations, events, awards, fellowships and grants, services, etc., for the publishing trade in the U.S. and Canada; includes foreign publishers with U.S. offices. Geographic location, type, and subject indexes for U.S. publishers. Directory of organizations and individuals included in the text (with phone numbers and addresses).

O'Dwyer's Directory of Corporate Communications. J.R. O'Dwyer Co., Inc., New York, NY, annual.
Lists public relations/communications people at companies and associations, including foreign embassies, federal government departments, bureaus, agencies, and commissions. Industry and geographic indexes to corporations; geographic index to associations. Includes foreign listings (mostly Canadian).

O'Dwyer's Directory of Public Relations Firms. J.R. O'Dwyer Co., Inc., New York, NY, annual.
Alphabetical listing of public relations firms and PR departments of advertising agencies and their branches; entries include principal executives and clients. Specialty, geographic, and client indexes. Includes firms and branches located outside the U.S.

Photographer's Market: Where & How to Sell Your Photographs. Michael Willins, editor. Writer's Digest Books, Cincinnati, OH, annual.
Introductory chapters on "The Business of Photography," followed by a classified listing of the markets, from advertising to stock photo agencies. Includes interviews with professionals in the field. Lists art/photo representatives, contests, and workshops. Bibliography. Glossary. First markets, subject, and general indexes.

Regional Theatre Directory. Jill Charles, compiler and editor. Theatre

Directories, Dorset, VT, annual.

Geographically arranged listings of theater companies and dinner theaters, with employment and internship information for performers, designers, technicians, and managers. Lists service organizations and resources, with a brief appendix on the employment process. Alphabetical index of theaters and index of "specialty" companies.

Songwriter's Market: Where & How to Market Your Songs. Cindy Laufenberg, editor. Writer's Digest Books, Cincinnati, OH, annual.

Introductory chapters on "The Business of Songwriting," followed by a classified listing of the markets, from advertising to record producers. Includes interviews with music business professionals who offer insights and advice. Lists organizations, workshops, contests and awards, and publications. Glossary. Indexed.

Standard Directory of Advertisers: The Advertiser Red Book. National Register Publishing, New Providence, NJ, 2 editions annually: classified and geographic (2 volumes each).

Lists companies engaged in national or regional advertising in the U.S. and Canada, with product and executive information. Lists advertising agencies and media used, amounts spent, etc. Each edition has company name, product categories by state, brand name, SIC, and personnel indexes. Cumulative supplements published in April, July, and October. Also available in CD-ROM format.

Standard Directory of Advertising Agencies. National Register Publishing, New Providence, NJ, twice yearly.

Lists advertising agencies, house agencies, media buying services, sales promotion agencies, and public relations firms. Gives size, dollar amount of billings, names of executives, and in many cases identifies accounts. Special market, geographic, and name indexes. Includes foreign agencies. Cumulative supplements published in April, July, and October. Also available in CD-ROM format.

Theatre Profiles: The Illustrated Guide to America's Nonprofit Professional Theatres. Theatre Communications Group, New York, NY, biennial.

Alphabetical listing of nonprofit resident theater companies, with staff, fiscal, and production information. Regional, name, and title indexes.

Writer's Market: Where & How to Sell What You Write. Mark Garvey, editor. Writer's Digest Books, Cincinnati, OH, annual.

Introductory chapters on the writing profession, followed by a classified listing of the markets, from book publishers to syndicates. Includes interviews with writers and editors. Lists organizations and contests and awards. Glossary, book publishers subject index, general index.

Business

Consultants and Consulting Organizations Directory: A Reference Guide to More Than 22,000 Concerns and Individuals Engaged in Consultation for Business, Industry, and Government. Janice McLean, editor. Gale Research Inc., Detroit, MI, annual. 2 volumes.
> Lists firms by field of consulting activity. Geographic, consulting activities, personal name, and consulting firms indexes. Also available online through the Human Resources Information Network.

The Corporate Finance Sourcebook. National Register Publishing, New Providence, NJ, annual.
> Classified listing of capital funding and management sources, including venture capital firms, banks, pension managers, and accounting firms. Firms, personnel, and geographic indexes.

Encyclopedia of Business Information Sources: A Bibliographic Guide to More Than 26,000 Citations Covering Over 1,100 Subjects of Interest to Business Personnel. James Woy, editor. Gale Research Inc., Detroit, MI, biennial.
> Includes print, online, organizational, etc., sources of information. An excellent resource for researching a particular business topic or industry.

Harvard Business School Career Guide: Finance. In Cooperation with the Harvard Business School Finance Club, distributed by the Harvard Business School Press, Boston, MA, 1994.
> Intended primarily for MBA students, this publication introduces the field and profiles firms that recruit for positions in finance. Includes a glossary, mailing list, and brief annotated bibliography.

Harvard Business School Career Guide: Management Consulting. In Cooperation with the Management Consulting Club, distributed by the Harvard Business School Press, Boston, MA, annual.
> Intended primarily for MBA students, this publication introduces the consulting field, and includes self-descriptions by a number of top firms. Includes a mailing list and a brief annotated bibliography.

The Insurance Almanac: Who What When and Where in Insurance. Donald E. Wolff, editor. The Underwriter Printing and Publishing Co., Englewood, NJ, annual.
> Lists brokers, adjusters, companies, officials, and related organizations, with names of principals. Indexed.

National Directory of Corporate Public Affairs. Arthur C. Close, J. Valerie Steele, and Michael E. Buckner, editors. Columbia Books, Inc., Washington, DC, annual.
> Alphabetical listing of companies with public affairs programs, giving

people, addresses, and publications. Alphabetical listing of individuals engaged in public affairs programs. Industry and geographic indexes; geographical listing of contract lobbyists. List of corporate clients that have engaged professional lobbying assistance at the state level from law firms, government relations firms, and individual lobbying consultants.

Peterson's Job Opportunities in Business. Peterson's, Princeton, NJ, annual.
Profiles of corporate and government employers. Industry, geographic, and hiring needs indexes.

Pratt's Guide to Venture Capital Sources. Venture Economics, New York, NY, annual.
Excellent introductory section on the venture capital industry, followed by geographically arranged listings of venture capital companies in the U.S. Includes a separate listing of foreign venture capital firms. Company, name, industry preference, and stage preference indexes.

Sports Market Place. Richard A. Lipsey, editor. Sportsguide, Inc., Princeton, NJ, annual with supplement and five newsletter updates per year.
Lists associations, teams, publications, broadcasters, promoters, suppliers, executive search firms, etc. Product, brand name, executive, and geographic indexes.

Standard & Poor's Register of Corporations, Directors, and Executives. Standard & Poor's Corp., New York, NY, annual, with supplements. 3 volumes.
Volume 1 lists U.S. corporations alphabetically, naming principal executives. Volume 2 lists directors and executives alphabetically, giving very brief biographical information where available. Volume 3 contains industrial, geographic, and corporate family indexes.

Standard & Poor's Security Dealers of North America. Standard & Poor's, New York, NY, semiannual.
Geographically arranged, with index of firms. Geographic listing of foreign offices and representatives. Lists North American exchanges and associations, North American securities administrators, and major foreign stock exchanges.

Thomson Bank Directory. Thomson Financial Publishing Inc., Skokie, IL, semiannual. 4 volumes.
Volumes 1 and 2 list banks geographically within North America and include names of officers and financial data. Bank and subject indexes. Volume 3 contains geographic listings of banks located outside North America. Country, bank, and subject indexes. Volume 4 provides information about principal correspondents for bank head offices throughout the world.

Training and Development Organizations Directory. Janice McLean, editor. Gale Research Inc., Detroit, MI, triennial.
> Profiles firms, institutes, etc. by content area. Geographic, training activities, personal name, and company indexes. Also available online through the Human Resources Information Network.

U.S. Real Estate Register. Barry, Inc., Wilmington, MA, annual.
> Four sections: real estate managers; profiles of companies, associations, government agencies, utilities, etc., involved in real estate or economic/industrial development; property digest; classified listings of services offered by the industrial/commercial real estate and economic/industrial development industries.

Education

The Handbook of Private Schools: An Annual Descriptive Survey of Independent Education. Porter Sargent Publishers, Inc., Boston, MA, annual.
> Geographically arranged listing of leading private schools, with separate listings for schools abroad, schools for the underachiever, etc. Index of schools. "Features" index (ungraded curriculum, single-sex, military program, international baccalaureate, etc.).

National Directory of Alternative Schools. Michael Traugot, editor. The National Coalition of Alternative Community Schools, Santa Fe, NM, biennial.
> Geographic listing of schools in the U.S. and other countries. Includes lists of homeschooling organizations, alternative colleges and universities, resources, and affiliated organizations. Indexed.

Private Independent Schools. Bunting and Lyon, Inc., Wallingford, CT, annual.
> Geographically arranged listing includes American programs in other countries and U.S. territories; separate section for summer programs, including sports, the arts, etc. Index of schools. "Classification Grid" by state serves as a quick reference for identifying specific program features.

Government, Health, Human Services, and Law

The Almanac of American Politics. Michael Barone and Grant Ujifusa. National Journal, Washington, DC, annual.
> Contains basic information on elections, individuals, and events, from the Presidency and Congress through the state level. Detailed data on congressional districts and their representatives, and separate chapters on demographics and campaign finance. Indexed.

Carroll's Federal Directory. Carroll Publishing, Washington, DC, bimonthly.
Telephone numbers, names, addresses, and titles for individuals in the
executive, legislative, and judicial branches. Keyword index. Also
available on disk and in CD-ROM format.

Carroll's Federal Regional Directory. Carroll Publishing, Washington, DC,
semiannual.
Information on federal regional offices, home state offices of members of
Congress, key personnel of federal courts, and contacts for military bases.
Name, keyword, and geographic indexes. Also available on disk and in
CD-ROM format.

Carroll's Municipal Directory. Carroll Publishing, Washington, DC, semiannual.
Lists municipalities in two groups: those with populations over 15,000,
and those with populations under 15,000. Includes cities, towns, town-
ships, villages, and Census Designated Places, as well as a listing of
national and state municipal associations. Alphabetical listing of executives. Geographic index.

Carroll's State Directory. Carroll Publishing, Washington, DC, three times
yearly.
State-by-state listing of government officials, including telephone numbers. Separate section for legislative committees and officers. Lists state
supreme courts. Personal name and keyword indexes.

Congressional Staff Directory. Ann L. Brownson, editor. Staff Directories,
Ltd., Mount Vernon, VA, semiannual.
Information on key personnel of the legislative branch, committees, and
subcommittees. Congressional staff biographies; keyword index; index of
individuals.

*Congressional Yellow Book: Who's Who in Congress Including Committees
and Key Staff.* Leadership Directories, Inc., New York, NY, quarterly.
Profiles members of Congress and congressional committees; includes
information on aides and congressional support agencies (such as the
Library of Congress). Staff and organization indexes. Also available in
CD-ROM format.

*Federal Regional Yellow Book: Who's Who in the Federal Government's
Agencies, Courts, Military Installations and Service Academies Outside of
Washington, DC.* Leadership Directories, Inc., New York, NY, semiannual.
Lists the departments, independent agencies, Congressional support agen-
cies, and U.S. courts. Geographic, name, and organization indexes. Also
available in CD-ROM format.

Federal Yellow Book: Who's Who in Federal Departments and Agencies.
Leadership Directories, Inc., New York, NY, quarterly.
> Arranged by department or agency, lists names and telephone numbers of
> top people in the executive branch of the federal government. Indexed.
> Also available in CD-ROM format.

Law and Legal Information Directory. Steven Wasserman, Jaqueline Wasserman
O'Brien, and Bonnie Shaw Pfaff, editors. Gale Research Inc., Detroit, MI,
biennial. 2 volumes.
> Organizations, courts, agencies, schools, funding sources, libraries, research
> centers, publications, etc., arranged by category. Some sections have indexes.

Martindale-Hubbell Law Directory. Martindale-Hubbell, New Providence,
NJ, annual.
> Profiles lawyers and law firms geographically. Includes a services and
> suppliers section for each state or territory. Also available online and in
> CD-ROM format.

Municipal Yellow Book: Who's Who in the Leading City and County Govern-
ments and Local Authorities. Leadership Directories, Inc., New York, NY,
semiannual.
> Three sections: cities, counties, and authorities. Geographic, population,
> and staff indexes. Also available in CD-ROM format.

National Directory of Children, Youth & Families. Marion L. Peterson.
Longmont, CO, annual.
> Part 1 is a state-by-state listing of public and private services and agencies.
> Part 2 lists federal and national organizations and clearinghouses. Part 3
> is a buyer's guide to specialized services and products.

National Directory of Private Social Agencies. Croner Publications, Inc.,
Jericho, NY, 1993, with monthly supplements.
> Geographically arranged, with the index of services. Very little informa-
> tion beyond address and telephone numbers, but it identifies some fairly
> obscure services.

Peterson's Job Opportunities in Health Care. Peterson's, Princeton, NJ, annual.
> Profiles of corporate and government employers. Industry, geographic,
> and hiring needs indexes.

Public Interest Profiles, 1992-1993. Foundation for Public Affairs. Congressional Quarterly, Inc., Washington, DC, 1992.
> Profiles public interest and public policy organizations. Arranged by field
> of interest; includes think tanks. Good coverage of each group provides
> budget information, staff size, operating method, publication lists, etc.
> Group, subject, and name indexes.

State Yellow Book: Who's Who in the Executive and Legislative Branches of the 50 State Governments. Leadership Directories, Inc., New York, NY, quarterly.
Includes state profiles and intergovernmental organizations. Subject and name (by state) indexes. Also available in CD-ROM format.

The United States Government Manual. Office of the Federal Register, National Archives and Records Administration, Washington, DC, annual.
Official handbook of the U.S. government; describes departments and agencies, lists key personnel, and provides organization charts. Name and subject/agency indexes. Includes information on quasi-official agencies, international organizations in which the U.S. participates, boards, committees, and commissions. The place to start for information on the federal government.

Washington Information Directory. Congressional Quarterly Inc., Washington, DC, annual.
Classified arrangement of information services in the public and nonprofit sectors in the Washington area, including names of officials and brief statement of mission. Name and subject indexes.

Washington 94: A Comprehensive Directory of the Key Institutions and Leaders of the National Capital Area. Columbia Books, Inc., Washington, DC, annual.
Classified arrangement of institutions, law firms, the media, governmental units, and other organizations in Washington. Index of organizations and individuals. (Title changes with year.)

Washington Representatives: Who Does What for Whom in the Nation's Capital. Columbia Books, Inc., Washington, DC, annual.
Alphabetical listing of individuals who work for American trade associations, professional societies, labor unions, corporations, and special interest groups, etc., followed by an alphabetical listing of companies and organizations. Subject and foreign interest indexes.

Science and Technology

The Biotechnology Directory: Products, Companies, Research and Organizations. J. Coombs and Y.R. Alston. Stockton Press, New York, NY, annual.
Three parts: international organizations; companies, university & government departments, institutes, and societies (arranged by country); buyer's guide to products and services.

Conservation Directory: A List of Organizations, Agencies, and Officials Concerned with Natural Resource Use and Management. National Wildlife Federation, Washington, DC, annual.

Includes international, national, and regional commissions and organizations, as well as U.S. and Canadian government and citizens' groups. Lists colleges and universities, conservation/environment offices of foreign governments, additional resources, etc. Subject and name indexes.

Corporate Technology Directory. Corporate Technology Information Services, Inc., Woburn, MA, annual. 4 volumes.

Alphabetically profiles U.S. companies that manufacture or develop high-technology products. Company name, geographic, non-U.S. parent company, technology, "who makes what," and SIC code indexes.

Directory of American Research and Technology: Organizations Active in Product Development for Business. R.R. Bowker, New York, New Providence, NJ, annual.

Alphabetical listing of nongovernment facilities involved in research and development, including subsidiaries. Information on staff and research fields. Geographic, personnel, and classified indexes. Subject guide to R&D activities.

The Directory of Massachusetts High Technology Companies. Mass Tech Times, Inc., Woburn, MA, annual.

Lists manufacturing, research, engineering, consulting, and software firms. Names key personnel. Product and geographic indexes.

Gale Environmental Sourcebook: A Guide to Organizations, Agencies, and Publications, 2nd ed. Donna Batten, editor. Gale Research Inc., Detroit, MI, 1994.

Arranged by type of organization. Includes a section on scholarships and awards, glossary, and lists of endangered and threatened wildlife and plants. Alphabetic and subject indexes.

Peterson's Job Opportunities in Engineering and Technology. Peterson's, Princeton, NJ, annual.

Profiles of corporate and government employers. Industry, geographic, and hiring needs.

Peterson's Job Opportunities in the Environment. Peterson's, Princeton, NJ, annual.

Profiles of corporate and government employers. Industry, geographic, and hiring needs indexes.

Handbooks

The Academic Job Search Handbook. Mary Morris Heiberger and Julia Miller Vick. University of Pennsylvania Press, Philadelphia, PA, 1992.

Five sections: what you should know before you start; planning and timing your search; written materials for the search; conducting the search; after you take the job. Lists national job-listing sources and scholarly professional associations.

Career Planning Guide for International Students, 2nd ed. Kerry Santry, Jane Sommer, and Pam Wells, editors. International Careers Consortium, Boston, MA, 1993.
Discusses career planning, the job-search process (in both the U.S. and abroad), immigration and legal issues, work in the U.S., and return to the home culture. Lists resources.

How to Put Your Book Together and Get a Job in Advertising. Maxine Paetro. The Copy Workshop, Chicago, IL, 1990.
A guide to compiling a portfolio, with job-hunting hints specific to advertising; includes interviews with creative people in the field.

How to Survive without Your Parents' Money: Making It from College to the Real World. Geoff Martz. Villard Books, New York, NY, 1993.
This general career guide has chapters on career exploration, the job hunt, networking, living on one's own, careers in the arts, etc. Brief bibliography.

The Insider's Guide Series. Surrey Books, Chicago, IL, 1992-1994.
"How to Get a Job in" ten U.S. cities, Europe, and the Pacific Rim. Each book includes lists of employers, contacts, and job-hunting advice.

The New Network Your Way to Job and Career Success: Turn Contacts into Job Leads, Interviews, and Offers, 2nd ed. Ronald L. Krannich and Caryl Rae Krannich. Impact Publications, Manassas Park, VA, 1993.
Includes a list of associations and networking organizations, along with advice on how to make and maintain professional contacts. Chapters on electronic networking services and the most effective use of resources. Bibliography. Indexed.

The Overnight Job Change Strategy. Donald Asher. Ten Speed Press, Berkeley, CA, 1993.
Includes chapters on identifying and developing raw leads, effective use of the telephone, negotiating the job offer, and troubleshooting failed searches. Bibliography.

A Ph.D. Is Not Enough: A Guide to Survival in Science. Peter J. Feibelman. Addison-Wesley Publishing Co., Reading, MA, 1993.
Includes chapters on choosing a thesis adviser or postdoctoral position, preparing oral presentations and grant proposals, publishing, getting funded, etc.

Successful Job Search Strategies for the Disabled: Understanding the ADA.
Jeffrey G. Allen. John Wiley & Sons, Inc., New York, NY, 1994.
> Gives an overview of the ADA. Discusses employment practices, self-assessment, resumes and cover letters, job leads, references, disclosure, interviewing accommodations, enforcement, etc. Resource list.

Take Charge: A Strategic Guide for Blind Job Seekers. Rami Rabby and Diane Croft. National Braille Press Inc., Boston, MA, 1989.
> Available in print, Braille, cassette, IBM disk, and VersaBrailleII editions, this book offers valuable advice on self-assessment, career exploration, the job hunt, and surviving on the job. Much of the information is appropriate for any job seeker, not just those with visual and/or other disabilities. Lists resources.

Indexes

Business Periodicals Index. H.W. Wilson Co., Bronx, NY, monthly, except August, with annual cumulations.
> Indexes English-language business periodicals, with a separate listing of citations to book reviews. A good way to look up current information on potential employers, assuming you have access to the periodicals indexed.

Current Index to Journals in Education. Oryx Press, Phoenix, AZ, under contract with the U.S. Office of Education's Educational Resources Information Center (ERIC), monthly, with semiannual cumulations.
> Indexes articles in nearly 800 education and education-related journals. Subject, author, and journal content indexes. Also available in microfiche and CD-ROM format.

F&S Index United States. Information Access Co., Foster City, CA, monthly.
> Indexes financial publications, business-oriented newspapers, trade magazines, and special reports. Two sections: industries & products; companies.

PAIS International in Print. Public Affairs Information Service, Inc., New York, NY, monthly, 3 of which are cumulations, with annual cumulation.
> Indexes public and social policy materials issued worldwide in six languages (English, French, German, Italian, Portuguese, and Spanish). Covers a variety of formats: periodicals, books, government documents, serials, pamphlets, reports, and some microfiche publications. Arranged by subject. Also available online and in CD-ROM format.

The Readers Guide to Periodical Literature. The H.W. Wilson Co., Bronx, NY, 16 times a year, cumulated annually.
> Author and subject index to general interest English-language periodicals,

including titles in the arts, business, education, government, health, music, and science. Includes a listing of citations to book reviews.

Skills Development

Made Simple Books. Doubleday, New York, NY, various dates.
Self-study guides on nearly 35 subjects, including accounting, statistics, desktop publishing, languages, Wall Street, and small business topics.

Schaum's Outline Series. McGraw-Hill Book Co., New York, NY.
Numerous titles in the fields of accounting, business, computers, languages, mathematics, statistics, etc. Each outline gives basic theory, definitions, and sample problems.

Chapter 5

TRANSITION

RESPONDING TO A JOB OFFER

When you get offered a job, whether during an interview or a telephone call, respond with enthusiasm, but do not accept the offer. Express your pleasure at receiving the offer, your interest in the job and the company, and ask for time to make your decision. Hopefully, you have anticipated the possibility of a job offer and have some idea how much time you would like to have to make your decision. Some of the questions that you may want to ask yourself are the following:

- Is this the right job for you? What are the positives and negatives of this opportunity?
- Are you waiting to hear from other employers?
- Is the salary acceptable?

Is This the Right Job for You?

You were selective about which positions you applied for and have been weighing the positive and negative aspects of the job as you gathered more information. During your research, you screened out those positions which did not appeal to you or which were unsuitable for one reason or another. The employment interview provided you with a firsthand glimpse of the employer and gave you the opportunity to ask questions that you deemed important. It is likely that you would not have continued as a candidate if there were serious points of disagreement or if certain features of the job were totally unacceptable to you. Now that you have been offered the job, however, you want to evaluate carefully all the information you can learn about the position and the company.

Ask yourself some of the same questions you asked as you began your career exploration.

- Will this job challenge you to increase your skills and develop expertise?
- Is the work interesting and worthwhile?
- Do you like the work environment?
- Do you like the people?
- Is there opportunity to accomplish something?
- Is there opportunity for growth in the job?
- Is the geographic location one in which you want to live?
- Are the benefits (health insurance, vacation, and retirement) adequate?
- Is the salary acceptable?

Your positive answers to these questions should outnumber your negative ones. Although it is not possible to get everything you want in your first job, it should challenge you and provide the opportunity to learn.

Are You Waiting to Hear from Other Employers?

What you do about other employers depends on your current relationship to them. If you think that you would prefer to work for one of the other employers with whom you have interviewed, you should call to tell them that you have an offer and ask when they will be able to make their decision about your candidacy. If you are certain that you prefer the second company, you can tell them so, but if you are uncertain which company you prefer, say nothing, or if asked, say that you are still weighing the advantages of the jobs at each company.

If there are other employers that interest you, but you have not been interviewed by them, you will probably have to make a decision about this job offer before you can know the viability of the other possibilities. In that case, you have to evaluate this job on its own merit with regard to the opportunity that it offers to build your expertise and your professional reputation. If you turn down a job offer, recognize that you may not get another for some time.

Is the Salary Acceptable?

Salary will probably figure in your deliberations. You will need to make a certain amount of money to support yourself, to pay off educational debts you may have accumulated, to afford some of your favorite leisure activities, and to set aside a bit for those inevitable unforeseen expenses which are a part of life. Of course, you will need to have realistic expectations in terms of lifestyle. On the income from your first job, you cannot expect to be able to afford the housing, leisure activities, wardrobe, vacations, and family that you dream about having someday. It is the salary expectation over time that you want to take into consideration.

Your personal needs and desires have little influence on the salary a prospective employer offers you. His offer will usually be based on what he has determined is a fair price based on the industry, the organization's internal structure and salary schedule, the geographic location, your qualifications and experience, and what he perceives to be your potential value to the organization. With so many variables, how do you evaluate the fairness of an offer? You do what you have been doing from the start of your career exploration: research, research, research!

Where Do You Get Salary Information?

You are already familiar with resources that can give you some idea of what salary to expect. *The Occupational Outlook Handbook, The American Almanac of Jobs and Salaries*, and other career books give approximate salary ranges. The professional journals you have been reading are likely to publish articles or studies on compensation in their respective fields. Professional associations often conduct surveys of their members and might provide some information about salary ranges. The help wanted ads in newspapers and journals will sometimes list ranges for positions similar to the one you are considering, in a variety of geographic locations.

Do remember, however, that the size of the organization can make a big difference. Large organizations may pay slightly more, but have comparatively rigid salary scales and performance review schedules; small employers may reward outstanding performance more readily with bonuses and pay increases, but may not offer the same employee benefits as a large employer. Increasing numbers of employers are developing compensation structures based on skills and expertise or on productivity, instead of on seniority.

Members of your network can be an excellent source of information about salaries within their respective firms and a particular industry or profession. Your career advisers will probably know the approximate salary schedules of their competitors and any changes that are being considered in the compensation structure. It is important to remember during your investigation that you are seeking an equitable range, not a definite figure. You want to feel that you are being compensated fairly for the work that you will be doing.

When Do You Raise the Money Question?

As a rule, salary is one of the last items to be discussed, if it is at all, in the interviewing phase of job hunting. This usually works to your advantage, because you will have had an opportunity to demonstrate your potential value to the employer. Sometimes salary is mentioned only when a job offer is made; other times it is one of the first items on an interviewer's agenda. In any case, you should have gathered information about salary ranges from the literature and from your advisers so that you have some idea about what is an acceptable range to you. That way you will be prepared when the discussion of salary takes place.

Accepting a Job Offer

If you are offered a position over the telephone and salary is not mentioned, you should ask. Ordinarily, after you have expressed your pleasure at receiving the offer and your positive interest in the organization, the employer will tell you that you will be receiving a letter detailing the offer and giving specifics of the job description, salary, and benefits as appropriate, or that he would like to schedule a conference with you to discuss such specifics. If the employer does not tell you which to expect, you should ask. A job offer should be confirmed in writing or personal conference.

A job offer should also be accepted in writing or a personal conference. If there are any details that you wish to negotiate, you should plan to do this in a personal conference. Before you raise any details of the job offer for discussion, be sure that you make clear the level of your interest in the job. If the settlement on these details will make the difference in whether you accept the job, say so. On the other hand, if you plan to accept the job, but you would like to explore the possibility of accommodation on specific details, make that clear. Be careful not to damage your relationship with your new employer before you even start to work. As suggested in Chapter 4, an alternative structure of your job may be easier to arrange after the employer knows your work.

Do not accept a job offer unless you are ready to commit yourself to that employer. When you accept an offer, you should withdraw your name from all other applications. Employers within an industry or field communicate with one another, and reneging on the acceptance of one job to take another may damage your reputation throughout the industry or field.

MANAGING YOUR FIRST DAYS ON THE JOB

Starting a new job is an exciting adventure. There is a great deal to learn. Every organization has its own customs, priorities, and rewards; every supervisor is a unique individual. Your first days are a time for observing, listening, reading, asking questions, seeking guidance, and getting to know your fellow workers.

Before You Start

If there is a lapse of time between when you accept the job offer and when you start, use this time to continue your research about the company from the daily news and the professional literature. This is an appropriate time to get in touch with the members of your network to thank them and tell them about the job you have accepted. They may have knowledge about your company that will be helpful to you.

This is also a time to get your personal life in order. Review your wardrobe to make sure that you have clothes that you will feel comfortable wearing in this new environment. If you must move or you want to change your housing, try to get this completely taken care of before you start your new job. If there are family visits or trips that you want to take, schedule them before you start work if you can afford the time or expense. In other words, try to have your personal life in order, so that you are ready to give top priority to getting the right start on your job.

Learning the Corporate Culture

Every organization has its own culture consisting of value systems, recognition systems, expected behavior patterns, and formal and informal communication networks. The value system is expressed in the president's letter in the annual report, in the speeches of the CEO, or in who gets selected for recognition or promotion.

The values of an organization guide the decisions of managers, influence the behavior of the workers, and determine the reward system. Individuals selected for special recognition because they have demonstrated outstanding achievement in a valued activity are sometimes referred to as company heroes. Recognition may or may not include promotion, but it is always public: for example, in such awards as the "Programmer of the Month" or membership in the "100% Club." Observing who gets recognized and for what accomplishments gives you insight into the organization's values.

Expected behavior patterns are often expressed as "the way we do things around here." Styles of interaction and procedures for getting things done are tied to the company culture and are usually best learned by observation. You will probably find that almost everyone around you is willing to help you learn, if you ask. It is wiser to ask for advice on procedures than to plunge ahead and damage your working relationships by inappropriate behavior.

The informal communication network provides "insider information" and interpretations of official decisions and events in the organization. To get plugged into the informal channels of communication, you need only be a good listener. If you do a lot of listening and resist expressing opinions during your first days, you will gain a great deal of insight into the organization and learn who are reliable sources of useful information.

Becoming a Member of the Organization

When you start a new job, you are joining a team. Members of the team rely on each other in order to get their work done. As the new employee in the group, you should make an effort to get to know everyone by name: your peers, the supervisors, the secretaries, the technicians, the guards, everyone!

Building strong working relationships with your colleagues is different from developing personal friendships. Your coworkers do not need to know your life history to feel acquainted. Friendships with colleagues are built primarily on sharing work-related interests and activities. Time for conversation is limited during the working day, and you will want to make the most of opportunities to increase your understanding of who does what and how work gets done.

Learning Your Job

Your supervisor is the person who defines your job, assigns your work, and evaluates your performance. You will probably meet with him the first day and you should be prepared with questions that will clarify your responsibilities and his expectations. Your supervisor may be the person who trains you, or he may designate someone else to instruct you. If your supervisor is busy and does not have much time to help you get started, you should ask him whom you should turn to with your questions.

Every job has menial and repetitive work. Beware of thinking someone else should wait on you. You should be willing to undertake any of the tasks that are necessary to get the job done, whether they are photocopying, word processing, or answering phones. Pitch in and do your part to help the team run smoothly.

Making a Commitment

Starting a new job is like moving to a foreign country. You have to learn the language, customs, and mores, as well as learning how to do your job. The first few weeks can be difficult. From time to time you may question whether this is the right job for you, but be patient. If your job represents a new challenge to you, you may not feel as if you are measuring up to your expectations for six months or a year, since a challenging job takes a while to learn. Commit your best effort for a year and prove to yourself and your employer that you are worthy of his trust and respect.

LOOKING AHEAD

When you are no longer learning on your job, you should look for new challenges. You may not have to look far. One option is to redesign how you get your work done. If you can fulfill your assigned responsibilities and take on new tasks, that might provide opportunities to increase your skills and enhance your reputation for being productive. One of the ways to develop your career is to enlarge the job you have. If your salary is based on skills or on productivity, you can increase your salary while improving your professional reputation.

If you have developed relationships with people in various parts of the company, you will be able to learn where there is turnover in staff or new product developments that might provide potential opportunities for you. If career opportunities with your present employer do not meet your expectations, you know the process and have the skills for searching for new opportunities. If your talents and aspirations develop in such a way that your interest in your present career decreases, you know how to engage in career research to move on to something new. With your skill in the career development process, you are prepared to forge your own career.

BUILDING AND MAINTAINING NETWORKS

To support the ongoing development of your career, you need connections with people with whom you share career-related interests. Your networks should include people in your industry and related industries, people with similar work experience and different work experiences, people of your own age and people who are your senior. Your networks should include people who work for the same employer and others who are employed in other companies or organizations.

Your relationship with the people in your network is built around common professional interests. Because of the work that each of you do or have done in the past, you have information, ideas, news, and contacts to share. The people in your networks are your professional friends; they may or may not be friends whom you see socially evenings or weekends.

There are many ways that you can keep in touch with the people in your network. You can communicate by telephone, by letter, by email, by meeting for lunch—whatever suits the two of you. The frequency of your contacts may vary depending upon what's going on in your professional lives or your industries. When either of you is anticipating or undergoing change, you may want to be in more frequent contact. However, having a good conversation at least once a year during which you each have a chance to share important happenings in your work lives and to discuss issues that concern you is probably enough to maintain your connection.

Joining Professional Associations

Every time that you are with a group you have the opportunity to meet new people and to learn about their work. One of the best ways of making new contacts is by joining professional associations. Becoming a member of professional associations provides the opportunity to expand your network and to increase your knowledge of the profession. You will want to select which associations you want to join. Usually there is a specific association that people in your industry or profession belong to, but there also may be associations with diverse memberships that would provide the opportunity to greatly expand your horizons. Examples of these include the National Association of Female Executives and your local Chamber of Commerce.

If you attend meetings at regular intervals, you will have the opportunity to stay in touch with friends and to meet new people. It may take conscious effort to make a few new friends at every meeting; it is so easy to visit only with those you have already met. Expanding your network of friends requires that you circulate at the beginning of the meeting or at the reception.

If you take on leadership positions, it will enable you to develop closer relationships with people in the organization because you will be working together. It will also give you an opportunity to develop management skills which will add to your employability.

PLANNING YOUR FINANCES

Personal financial planning is the topic of numerous books, radio and television broadcasts, journal articles, workshops, and seminars. It is also a major industry: according to the *Encyclopedia of Associations*, the

Institute of Certified Financial Planners has 7,500 members nationwide and an annual budget of $2,600,000; the International Association for Financial Planning has 25,000 members in ten countries and a budget of $10,000,000! With so much attention being paid to the subject in the world at large, you may want to take a more personal view in terms of your own financial situation.

To begin with, the whole concept of financial planning revolves around one very basic tenet: what goes out must be less than or equal to what comes in. This sounds simple, but as anyone who has ever balanced a checkbook will tell you, there seem to be infinitely more ways to diminish one's cash on hand than to augment it. The negative numbers that are acceptable in the field of mathematics will not favorably impress your bank.

It is important to examine carefully and to anticipate what your actual expenses will be. This sounds easier than it is. Although you will be able to calculate your regular monthly costs with some accuracy, it is the occasional, unanticipated extras and the annual lump-sum payments for certain items that are guaranteed budget breakers.

Start-up costs when establishing yourself in a new city or when building a professional wardrobe can also be disastrous to what you thought was the most carefully balanced budget. You need to be realistic when setting your priorities and when calculating what things really cost. You will also need to make sure you take into account just about anything that is likely to cost you money. The lists that follow are intended to help you do just that.

Monthly expenditures: housing (rent or mortgage and real estate tax payment, renters/homeowners insurance); utilities (electricity, gas, telephone, cable, online computer service, water); heat/cooling (if not included in rent or utilities); transportation (public transportation, taxis, car rentals) or automobile expenses (monthly payment, insurance, parking, tolls, fuel/oil, excise tax, registration, car wash, routine maintenance); food; dry cleaning/laundry; toiletries and household supplies; educational loans; entertainment (restaurants, movies, videotape rentals, sporting events, concerts, etc.); charitable contributions; postage (for paying all your bills!); etc.

Annual expenditures: professional memberships or dues; subscriptions; gifts (birthdays, anniversaries, etc.); annual credit card fees; travel (vacations, visits to friends/family, etc.).

In addition to the above, certain obligations will be met for you through payroll deductions: federal, state, and municipal taxes; social security or other preretirement contributions; health insurance premiums; any life/disability insurance or savings/supplemental pension plan through your employer.

By now, you are probably wondering what is left and how to cover such luxuries as clothing for your new job or a few items to furnish your rather empty new living quarters (not to mention an occasional bottle of champagne to celebrate your career advancement and that of your friends). One way to keep yourself reasonably solvent is to prioritize your expenditures, especially when you are starting out. You should also identify the items that are likely to take the biggest bite out of your resources (e.g., rent and transportation), and find ways to reduce them or keep them under control.

For instance, you may need to have several roommates to share housing and utility expenses or join a carpool rather than drive to work every day. Some employers will subsidize public transportation expenses; find out if this is an option where you work. Learn to shop for food and household supplies at supermarkets and discount stores rather than convenience stores and gourmet shops; you will pay less, especially if you watch for sales. Try to pay your credit card bills in full each month; otherwise, the finance charges will put a serious dent in your budget.

This is probably a good place to warn about the dangers of credit cards. It is very easy to place yourself in a great deal of debt in a very short period of time. Remember: that piece of plastic represents a commitment on your part to pay a bill. This bill will appear in your mailbox much sooner than you would like; to make matters worse, it will be accompanied by many others. That impulse purchase you made on your lunch hour will begin to transform itself into a millstone.

Last, but not least, you should get into the habit of saving a portion of each paycheck. The amount is not important, although the more you can set aside, the better your financial situation will be. A payroll deduction plan, if available to you, is a good way to insure that your good intentions become a reality. For instance, if you wanted to put $1,000 a year in savings, you would have $19.25 deducted from your weekly paycheck. If you put this in a savings account, it would not earn a very high interest rate, but you would be making progress toward savings for graduate school or for a down payment on a car or a house, or to cover your expenses during a period of unemployment.

For your longer-term financial goals, if you could invest $1,000 a year in a Tax Deferred Annuity (TDA) and earn an average 10% rate of return (which is the historical average in the stock market), your savings would accumulate as follows:

After 5 years	$ 6,700
After 10 years	$ 17,500
After 15 years	$ 35,000
After 20 years	$ 63,000
After 25 years	$108,200

If you can put aside your savings and invest them, they will become an added source of income and greatly increase your financial assets over time.   The key to successful financial planning is to identify your investment goal, the amount of risk you can afford to take, and the time frame for achieving your goal. With so many options to choose from, you may wish to consult the books listed at the end of this chapter. They will help you navigate your way through the world of mutual funds, zero coupon bonds, certificates of deposit, annuities, stocks, and all the other investment vehicles that exist in the world of personal finance.

SOURCES

Planning Your Finances

Money, Banking, and Credit Made Simple. Merle E. Dowd. Doubleday, New York, NY, 1994.
    Basic guide to the banking and credit industries. Includes worksheets, glossary, and resource list. Indexed.

365 Ways to Save Money. Lucy H. Hedrick. Hearst Books, New York, NY, 1994.
    Money-saving tips arranged by category, from banking to utilities. Indexed.

Your First Financial Steps. Nancy Dunnan. Harper Perennial, New York, NY, 1995.
    Chapters on budgeting, getting and managing credit, finding affordable housing, minimizing living expenses, and financial considerations associ-

ated with marriage and live-in arrangements. Includes budget worksheets. Indexed.

Your Money or Your Life: How to Save Thousands on Your Health-Care Insurance. Donald Jay Korn. Collier Books, New York, NY, 1992.
Discusses how to assess one's health, disability income, and long-term-care insurance needs; offers suggestions on how to evaluate different types of plans. Glossary; indexed.

Chapter 6

CAREER DEVELOPMENT SKILLS

WRITING A RESUME

What Is a Resume?

Your resume is an evolving description of your experiences which documents and describes your skills and expertise. Each edition is a presentation designed for a specific audience and a specific purpose. As an outline of your accomplishments, your resume communicates your qualifications for employment.

The purpose of a resume is to introduce yourself to prospective employers. The objective is to present your skills and expertise clearly and succinctly so that the employer will want to interview you. The resume is also a record of your name, address, telephone number, and pertinent information, which you can leave with potential employers and which you can give to members of your network. You should always have an up-to-date edition of your resume, but you should reconsider its format and content anytime you undertake a new search.

The particular mix of qualifications that an employer is seeking will depend on the job to be filled. The more you know about what the employer is looking for, the better you can tailor your presentation so that it describes your most relevant skills and knowledge in language that the employer understands.

Your resume should communicate your general qualifications as well as your specific skills. In preparing descriptions of your academic achievements, student activities, and employment, make certain that you document your general skills, such as your ability to

- learn quickly
- adapt to new environments
- research, analyze, and solve problems
- initiate and develop new programs
- work collaboratively on a team
- lead a team
- follow instructions
- use time efficiently
- deal with ambiguity
- make decisions
- communicate effectively
- meet deadlines

Employers who have a job that they want done look for people who are enthusiastic, energetic, reliable, mature, productive, perceptive, intelligent, persistent, conscientious, and ambitious. Wouldn't you?

Preparing to Write Your Resume

Your resume should be designed for two types of reading: someone scanning your resume should glean your academic degrees, job titles, special experiences, or skills; someone reading your resume should learn valuable information about your achievements and gain an impression of your competencies and personal qualities.

Developing a good resume is a challenging task. The best resumes are usually a product of many drafts. Start by writing a comprehensive outline of all the experiences and information you might want to include. Use this outline as a reference while you experiment with a variety of formats and styles. Then select the most pertinent information from the outline and organize it so that the most important items stand out.

In order to develop a resume that communicates your qualifications, you need to understand what employers are seeking. Identify several prospective employers and find out what skills and knowledge they are looking for. Reading occupational and company literature gives you a good introduction to this information, but visiting a person at work so you can observe the functions, pace, interpersonal relationships, and work environment will allow you to assess firsthand what qualifications are most important.

Ask several different people to read and comment on drafts of your resume. Friends can tell you whether they think you have succeeded in communicating your strengths. Advisers can comment on the impression your resume makes and what they learn about you from it. When you interview career advisers to learn about occupations and gather job-hunting advice, ask them to critique your resume for its appropriateness to their field.

Career counselors can also help you identify what employers are looking for and what you have to offer. When you meet with a counselor, bring a draft or drafts of your resume and the comprehensive outline from which you have worked. This will make it easier for the counselor to help you design a presentation which communicates your qualifications effectively. If you don't have directly related experience, your career counselor can help you analyze the relevant skills that you have developed in your activities and work experiences and describe those skills in words that the employer will understand.

Professional resume-writing services will develop your resume for a fee, but they will not produce a resume that is a personal reflection of your experience and uniquely yours. Most of these services use a small number of standard formats and styles. Your resume will look like hundreds of other peoples' resumes and the employer will probably recognize that it is not your own work.

The following guidelines are distilled from many consultations about resumes with students, job hunters, and employers. Please read them carefully and then start experimenting with different formats and styles for your presentation.

Types of Resumes

The format that you choose for your resume should be the one which you think best communicates your qualifications. There are three basic types of resumes: chronological, functional/chronological, and functional.

The **chronological resume** presents information in reverse chronological order under each category, i.e., Education, Work Experience, Activities. For example, under Education you would list your latest academic degree or degree-in-progress first, then other degrees received previously, or study at other universities such as study abroad, and, finally, your secondary school, if relevant. Likewise, under Experience you would list your current or most recent job first and continue in reverse chronological order, listing both your summer and term-time work and volunteer experiences. For consistency's sake, entries under additional sections such as Activities or Travel should also list the most recent experience first.

Some chronological resumes list the dates of each experience in the left margin. This is not required; dates can be listed anywhere. In fact, the left margin is prime space that can often be used more effectively to focus attention on job titles or places of employment, as in several of the sample resumes that follow. You can also attract the attention of the reader to the jobs or activities that you think are most relevant by writing a longer description of your responsibilities and accomplishments in them.

The chronological resume is the most common form of resume, especially for young people. Many employers prefer it because it catalogues work-related experiences in a straightforward fashion. At a glance, the employer learns your educational background, what you have done each summer, and what activities and work you have engaged in during each academic year.

The **functional/chronological** resume can be very effective in presenting specific career-related skills and achievements. For example, if you are applying to jobs in journalism, you could title a section, Journalism Experience. In this section you would list in reverse chronological order both paid and unpaid work and activities in which you have developed skills related to journalism. One entry might be "Editor, *The College Daily* — Covered all breaking news about faculty business. Met weekly with the Dean of the Faculty and attended all faculty meetings." Another entry might be "Reporter, *The Hometown Weekly* — Researched and wrote news stories as a summer replacement. Researched and wrote feature stories on the local toxic waste dump and summer youth recreation programs." Other functional categories that you might use include public relations, writing, research, teaching, leadership, management, computers, etc.

The entries within each section should be listed in reverse chronological order. Some positions might be listed in more than one section; for example, you might describe the teaching aspects of the position of Waterfront Director at a camp under the Teaching section, and the managerial/supervising aspects in a section presenting those skills. Overuse of double entries on this type of resume can seem very redundant. But when carried out successfully, the functional/chronological resume organizes the information that is most important to the employer and communicates that the applicant knows what types of skills he values.

The third type of resume, the **functional resume**, is more frequently used by midcareer people who are interested in changing careers. The first part of the resume lists accomplishments and/or qualifications in short, action-oriented statements which are usually highlighted with a bullet or asterisk. The second part provides a summary of the applicant's work history with dates, names of employers, and job titles. Sometimes a very impressive list of achievements, documented with information such as size of budget, number of employees, volume of sales, etc., can be extracted from years of work in a variety of jobs and presented in the functional part of the resume.

One difficulty with this type of resume is that, in order to assess the value or relevance of an accomplishment or activity, an employer may want to know the context in which it occurred. Therefore, it is important that you indicate the position with which each accomplishment is connected.

A fourth variation sometimes used by persons who are concerned about their age is to remove all the dates from their resumes. The dateless resume seems to bring out the Sherlock Holmes in many employers; their search for a clue which would indicate the applicant's age can distract them from appreciating his qualifications.

Electronic Resume

To facilitate their applicant tracking system, some employers now use a document scanner to "read" resumes into an electronic file. This computerized resume file can then be searched electronically to identify resumes which have words and phrases that indicate the candidate has the experience and the skills required for the current job opening. To find out whether an employer has an electronic tracking system, call the human resources department. If you learn that they are using electronic processing, ask for advice in the preparation of your electronic resume.

If your resume is going to be scanned into a computer and processed electronically, you should prepare a special version of it. To ensure a high level of accuracy during the scanning and searching processes, your **electronic resume** should be plain and bland in appearance, following these guidelines:

- Use a font size of 10-14 points.
- Use a popular typeface; sans serif is preferred.
- Remove all underlining, italics, script, and boldface.
- Use light-colored paper and black ink.
- Use relevant keywords (industry jargon) to describe your skills and experience. Insofar as you have the qualifications mentioned in the job description, use the same vocabulary in your resume.
- Avoid using abbreviations except very common ones such as degrees (BA, PhD) and states (MA, NY).
- Use a traditional resume structure; avoid graphics.
- Do not staple or fold your resume.
- Always send an original copy.

For a more complete discussion of the electronic resume, see the book *Electronic Resume Revolution* listed in the bibliography at the end of this chapter. The authors report that the keywords currently used by software programs to sort resumes are in noun form. This requires that you list your functions, accomplishments, and personal traits as nouns rather than as the action phrases recommended for paper resumes. Some employers report, however, that their software will search for keywords as nouns, verbs, or adjectives. It would be wise to ask members of your network about the current usage of computer processing of resumes in your targeted industry.

The electronic resume does not replace your regular resume. It is intended solely for scanning. When applying for employment, send copies of both your regular resume and electronic resume to the human resources department. When you write other executives in the firm or go to interviews, always use your regular resume.

Format

Most employers prefer a one-page resume. This preference is particularly strong in business. Employers in education, public service, and human services do not have as strong a preference for a one-page resume, although all employers want a well-organized and concise presentation of the most relevant information about you.

Remember that a resume is an example of your work. If you claim that you have organizational skills and the ability to communicate clearly and concisely, your resume should exemplify those traits.

Resume preparation requires careful thought and discipline. You must make judgments about what is most important and allot space accordingly. Descriptions of jobs and accomplishments must be brief and listings of activities selective. If you decide you cannot fit your resume on one page, try to arrange it so that the most important information is on the first page. Certain information that is often included in longer resumes, such as a list of publications or references, may be presented separately as attachments if you decide they are important to your application. Other attachments may include an annotated transcript, clippings, writing samples, a portfolio, and letters of recommendation.

As you experiment with different formats for your resume, make purposeful use of capitals, boldface, positioning, and spacing for emphasis and clarity. It is recommended that you **avoid using italics, underlining, and dot-matrix printers** because the resume may become less readable when it is copied or sent by fax.

If your resume is produced on a laser printer, you have many styles and sizes of type from which to choose. Choose one style to use throughout. Serif fonts are the easiest to read and therefore are usually preferred. Beware of using very small type. Anyone who has hundreds of resumes to read may pass right over a resume that is in very fine print or is very crowded.

White or ecru paper is preferred, and you should purchase matching envelopes and paper for your cover letters. Do not try to dazzle your potential employer by using brightly colored paper. It will overshadow your message and is very likely to land in the circular file.

Style

Style also communicates a message. Phrases with action verbs such as, "Designed data collection system. Analyzed data and prepared sixty-page report," give an efficient, goal-oriented impression. For some individuals, however, the flow of complete sentences is more suitable. Whichever style you choose, **be consistent**. Use the same sentence structure and format in every description.

The appearance of your resume also makes a strong impression. It should be neat, attractive, and easy to read. Graphically, your resume should not look crowded and should have one-inch margins on all four sides. Accuracy in use of language, information, and spelling is very important. If you do not have access to a word processor, hire someone who does. Check and double-check to make sure there are absolutely no errors, typos, or misspelled words. Employers report that they usually discard a resume when they find a misspelled word.

Content

It is expected that your resume will contain your name, address, telephone number, and information about your education and work experience. Other sections, titles, and arrangements are at your discretion.

Education and experience are usually presented in reverse chronological order. Within this structure you should give the most space to the most important experience. For example, the work experience which is most relevant to the job you are seeking or which demonstrates a skill valued in your chosen field should have the longest and most comprehensive description, as this will attract the reader's attention.

The discussion below is general advice. Remember that your resume should be designed to give the best presentation of your skills, expertise, and personal qualifications.

Name, Address, and Telephone. This is the most important information on the resume. Be sure this information is accurate so that employers can contact you! Usually it is centered and in capital letters at the top of the page. If you must give a temporary (school) address and home address, place your name at the top center and the addresses to the left and right. If you have an email address and/or a fax number, list them under your telephone number. It is not advisable to put your name in the upper left corner, as it will be obscured when a pile of resumes are clipped together.

Education. If you are a student or have recently completed an academic degree, it is best to put this section first. List your college or university degree or expected degree and date, concentration, subject of senior honors thesis (if written), and electives which are relevant to the type of employment you are seeking. Include selected honors if you have received recognition for outstanding academic work, but do not list your grade point average and SAT scores unless requested by the employer. Ph.D. students should list their department, area of interest, relevant electives, and selected honors. The dissertation topic may be included if it is of related interest.

If you have committed a lot of time to paid work during the academic year, you may want to insert a phrase such as "Worked 20 hours a week to help defray the cost of my education" in the Education section or at the end of the resume in a Personal section.

If you have studied abroad for one or two terms during the academic year or a summer, list that after your college. It does not matter whether you received graduation credit for your academic work abroad.

The secondary school is usually listed on undergraduate resumes. If you went to public high school, listing your secondary school tells employers where you are from. If you went to private school, listing your school may enable you to tap into an alumni network. Space devoted to honors and/or activities should depend on their contribution to the total message of your resume.

Work Experience. This section, which is usually the largest section, can be called Work Experience or Experience and will usually include all experience, paid and unpaid, and extracurricular activities which have given you the opportunity to develop the skills and qualifications that employers seek. You may mix paid and unpaid, part-time and full-time positions, but you should note in some way what the time commitment for each one was. Your experiences should be listed in reverse chronological order, drawing attention to your most important experience by the length of the description. For some people it is effective to list experience by career-related functions in order to highlight the quantity and quality of relevant experiences in the targeted field, such as public relations, journalism, or whatever.

The job title and organization should be listed prominently, but how you list them depends on what you wish to emphasize. If you were an intern, the job title of intern gives the reader little information, so you may want to create a functional title, such as research assistant or administrative assistant. If you were promoted to positions of greater responsibility in one organization over successive years or summers, make only one entry for that employer and list and describe each position, with the most responsible job title first. If your title has stayed the same, but you have completed increasingly complicated projects, you may want to describe your projects.

Under each listing, write a concise description of the functions you performed and the goals you achieved, using the vocabulary of the industry to which you are applying. Describe first the function that was most challenging and interesting, not necessarily the one at which you spent most of your time. Use action verbs such as those on the list at the end of this section to describe your accomplishments, and use numbers to communicate the magnitude of your achievements. Examples include the following:

- managed a $10,000 budget
- sold 20% more space than any other summer employee each month
- supervised installation of new computer system, adapted software, and trained 10 staff users
- recruited, trained, and supervised 25 volunteer tutors
- raised $5,000 to pay for new tutoring materials
- edited and prepared for publication a 200-page report on toxic waste
- made all arrangements for performances, transportation, and living accommodations for the Glee Club's six-week tour in Europe
- practiced four hours a day with the soccer team during fall term

Avoid the expression "Responsible for _____ ; this does not communicate that the tasks described were completed.

Listing the name of a reference person with each job is not necessary. If an employer wants letters of reference, he will ask for them. Most employers wait until they have narrowed the search to two or three candidates, and then they will ask you to provide telephone references— names of references whom the employer can call. Whenever you give the names of your references to an employer, be sure that you let them know that they might be receiving a call so that you can describe to them the position for which you are a candidate.

Activities. College activities can be listed and described under Experience, Activities, or most briefly under Personal Background, depending on how much emphasis and space you want to give them. If you have held leadership positions, initiated new programs, raised funds, sold advertising space, managed a large budget, or held any positions that have enabled you to develop employment-related skills, be sure you describe them. What activities you have chosen to participate in and what responsibilities you have carried out in each activity tell the employer something about what you like to do.

Always explain for the reader what the organization is, for example, "*The Independent*, a weekly news magazine" or "House Committee, student government in my residential unit of 350 students." If an organization has an acronym, write out the name of the organization the first time you mention it, with the acronym in parentheses.

Language Skills. Make a separate category to list language and computer skills. If you are a native speaker or fluent in the language, say so. If not, listing the number of years of study of the language in college is a good indicator of your proficiency. Other adjectives that are used include proficient, conversational, and spoken, but what level of ability each of these denotes is unclear. If you claim any of these, be prepared to be expected to converse in the language during your interview.

Computer Skills. These may be described with languages under the title Skills or may be listed separately. It is wise to indicate whether you have worked in an IBM or a Mac environment and to list some of the software programs you have used. If you are a computer programmer, describe your level of proficiency.

Travel. Experience traveling, working, or studying abroad should be mentioned on any resume either in a separate section or under Personal Background because it documents your ability to adjust to different cultures. If you are applying for work that is international, you should describe your foreign experience in detail.

Interests. Save at least one line for a list of avocational interests such as "reading science fiction, playing guitar, choral singing, and running." Even a brief list rounds out what you have told the reader about yourself and may establish an initial bond of common interest with an interviewer.

Personal Background. On a one-page resume you have had to leave out a great deal. This section may be used to mention information that you also consider important: "To help pay college expenses have worked every term delivering newspapers, washing dishes, bartending, driving a shuttle bus," "Lived in a small town in Ohio until I came to Harvard," "Born and grew up in New York City." (Where you spent your youth may be an important message to the employer.) Or, if you were born in another country, you might want to say, "Born and lived in Vietnam until I was twelve." Or, you might want to have a line about travel and a line about interests. If your address or place of birth raises any question about your citizenship or visa status, you should state what it is.

As you see in the samples in the following section, you do not want to have too many sections on your resume because they take up space and may segment the message too much.

Job Objective. The cover letter is the preferred place to state your job objective. This allows you to tailor it to each job application and to highlight and expand on relevant information from the resume. Only if you have a clearly defined employment goal should you write a job objective on the resume.

Summary of Qualifications. If you have some years of work experience, you may decide that you can communicate your qualifications best by leading off your resume with a list of your skills and expertise. Some Ph.D.'s who wanted to clarify their translatable skills for a nonacademic position have used this format effectively, as illustrated in the sample resume on page 158. A chronological work history may be included.

Action Words. This list may help you describe your accomplishments in your paid and unpaid work experiences.

Accelerated	Formed	Reduced
Accomplished	Formulated	Renegotiated
Achieved	Founded	Reorganized
Acted	Generated	Reported
Added	Guided	Represented
Administered	Halved	Researched
Advised	Headed	Resolved
Analyzed	Hired	Reversed
Appointed	Identified	Reviewed
Arranged	Implemented	Revised
Assembled	Improved	Scheduled
Assessed	Improvised	Selected
Audited	Increased	Served
Averted	Initiated	Settled

Bought
Broadened
Built
Centralized
Changed
Clarified
Classified
Collaborated
Competed
Compiled
Composed
Conducted
Computed
Conceived
Concluded
Constructed
Controlled
Coordinated
Counseled
Created
Defined
Delivered
Demonstrated
Designed
Determined
Developed
Doubled
Earned
Edited
Eliminated
Employed
Established
Evaluated
Examined
Executed
Expanded
Expedited
Fabricated
Followed

Inspected
Instituted
Instructed
Interviewed
Introduced
Invented
Launched
Lectured
Led
Located
Maintained
Managed
Marketed
Mediated
Minimized
Monitored
Motivated
Negotiated
Operated
Organized
Originated
Participated
Performed
Persuaded
Planned
Predicted
Prepared
Prevented
Processed
Programmed
Promoted
Proposed
Proved
Provided
Published
Purchased
Recommended
Recruited
Redesigned

Shaped
Simplified
Sold
Solved
Staffed
Started
Stimulated
Strengthened
Stretched
Structured
Studied
Summarized
Supervised
Supported
Surpassed
Surveyed
Synthesized
Taught
Terminated
Tested
Tightened
Traced
Trained
Translated
Trimmed
Tripled
Uncovered
Unified
Unraveled
Utilized
Verbalized
Verified
Visualized
Widened
Withdrew
Won
Worked
Wrote

Sample Resumes

The following sample resumes are fictionalized. They have been selected to represent a variety of formats and styles. We hope they will help you decide how you want to organize information, create emphasis, and describe your accomplishments. However, you should remember that your resume is a personal document. Develop a format and a style that best communicates your attributes for the job you seek.

Timothy A. Stern

school address:
353 Leverett Mail Center
Cambridge, MA 02138-6034
(617) 493-1808

home address:
8712 Southwest Avenue
Philadelphia, PA 19115
(215) 585-8122

Education

HARVARD UNIVERSITY
A.B. with honors expected in History and Economics in 1997. Named Winthrop Scholar for "outstanding qualities of leadership, as expressed by academic excellence, great athletic ability and performance, or extraordinary gifts in entrepreneurship, music, or the arts."

Experience

BUSINESS MANAGEMENT
* Assistant Manager of HSA Linen, an agency with annual revenue of $300,000 and profits of $90,000. Supervised all activities required to run a linen/laundry/dry cleaning business including: inventory control, sales, distribution, customer service, budgeting and accounting, advertising, quality control evaluation and implementation, contract negotiation, and interviewing, hiring, and training a staff of 10 employees.

VENTURE CAPITAL
* Intern for Strategic Capital Resources. Conducted market and tax code research. Identified and maintained personal contact with potential clients. Provided general assistance in writing business plans and offering memoranda. Assisted in the process of preparing businesses for expansion phases prior to initial public offerings.

ORGANIZATIONAL TEAM BUILDING
* Forged positive and productive liaison between management and personnel at HSA Linen.
* As a leader in the Freshman Outdoor Program, underwent extensive group dynamics training to assist in creating a cohesive bond among 8 incoming freshmen while leading a weeklong wilderness backpacking trip.
* Trained in leadership skills with Navy Reserve Officer Training Corps. Led NROTC human resources committee.
* As a Senior Leader in Boy Scouts of America, planned and executed weekly meetings, weekend outings, and training workshops for 4 years. Trained, evaluated, and counseled over 100 younger scouts.
* Earned the rank of Eagle Scout. Took command of 3 major community service projects. Coordinated with local organizations to raise funding and supplies. Planned project and supervised volunteers. Built erosion control system at C&O Canal National Historical Park as Eagle project.

TECHNICAL SKILLS
* Proficient in use of Quattro and Excel spreadsheets, WordPerfect and Microsoft Word word processing, Mac Draw graphics, and Platinum and Paradox databases.
* Provided professional service to top scientists by producing timely data analyses and graphic displays for Department of Defense physics laboratory. Co-authored report for use at the Pentagon.

Employment History

Strategic Capital Resources, Boston, MA (9/94-present)
Intern/Market Researcher
Harvard Student Agencies, Harvard University (2/94-2/95)
Assistant Manager of Linen
Career Orientation and Training for Midshipmen, Norfolk, VA (summer 1994)
NROTC summer service obligation
David Taylor Research Center, Carderock, MD (summer 1993)
Research Assistant/Data Analyst/Department of Defense Report Co-Author

Extracurricular Interests: play forward for Harvard Rugby Football Club; enjoy playing guitar and song writing; attend Harvard Memorial Church; enjoy backpacking and erging.

Comments: Timothy Stern has chosen to use a functional resume to organize the skills that he has developed through his work experiences and his activities. Note that he provides an employment history.

CECIL WANG

243 Adams Mail Center
Harvard University
Cambridge, MA 02138-5004
(617) 493-4067

Harvard Student Agencies, Inc.
53A Church Street
Cambridge, MA 02138
(617) 496-3412 or 495-3030

Education

HARVARD UNIVERSITY   Cambridge, MA
A.B. in History and Science expected in 1996. Harvard College Scholarship for
academic achievement. Dean's List. Coursework: American History, Biology,
Chemistry, Economics, English, European History, Math, Philosophy, Physics, Social
Studies. Worked over 20 hours per week every semester to defray cost of education.

ERIC HAMBER SECONDARY   Vancouver, BC
Class of '92 Valedictorian. Governor General Medal for superior achievement by state
government. Whittaker Scholarship for top student in graduating class. National Merit
Finalist. Head Coach of city champion junior varsity volleyball and badminton teams.

Work Experience

Manager   **HARVARD STUDENT AGENCIES**   Cambridge, MA
In charge of the linen agency of the largest student-run organization in the world.
Managed every aspect of the business from marketing, sales, and financial
operations to inventory, distribution, and personnel. Generated $300,000 in
revenue and $90,000 in net profit. Fall 1994 - present.

Operations   **EMPLOYMENT SOLUTIONS**   Cambridge, MA
Manager   Supervised the Human Resource Managers and assessed their progress in placing
over 600 students into job opportunities in the Harvard Dining Services. Restruc-
tured the placement process to increase yield by 25%. Fall 1994.

Business   **PWA CANADIAN AIRLINES**   Richmond, BC
Specialist   Researched mainframe file transfer systems for Technology Services division,
increasing efficiency by 20%. Interviewed 30 candidates for Computer Consultant
positions. Published weekly hardware and software review in journal. Summer 1993.

Telephone   **NATIONAL PAGETTE**   Vancouver, BC
Operator   Handled messages, processed data, and updated records for 200 clients. Spring 1993.

Activities

Business Editor   *Harvard Crimson* Business Department. Concentrated in advertising and sales. Sold 50% more ads than peers. Developed
weekly *Gourmet Guide* restaurant feature. Spring 1994 - Fall 1995.

Prefect   Harvard Prefecting Program. Supervised and advised resident
freshmen.   Fall 1994 - Spring 1995.

Editor   *Harvard Computer Review*. Wrote reviews of hardware and
software monthly.   Spring 1993 - Spring 1994.

Public   Asian American Association. Organized publicity for events
Relations   and planned staff meetings. Designed, coordinated, and distrib-
Officer   uted monthly newsletters. Provided liaison between AAA and
the Harvard Community.   Spring 1993 - Spring 1994.

Skills/Personal

Languages   Mandarin (fluent) and French (conversational).
Computers   IBM PC and MAC. Familiar with assorted word processing and database software.
Interests   Astronomy, chess, crew, dragon boats, horse racing, photography, and psychology.

Comments: By listing his job titles and leadership positions in the left margin, Cecil
Wang highlights his management and leadership experience. Under Education, he
lets us know that he attended high school in Canada, but he should also have
indicated his citizenship status because that is important information to employers.

DONALD ALLEN BICKELL

456 Eliot Mail Center
101 Dunster Street
Cambridge, MA 02138-6133
(617) 493-4433

Home Address:
2756 Elmwood Drive
St. Louis, MO 63146-3615
(314) 555-9587

EDUCATION

HARVARD COLLEGE   *Cambridge, MA*
Honors Double BA in Physics and Astrophysics expected in June '95. Received *summa cum laude* on senior thesis and won Goldberg Prize for Best Astro Thesis. Dean's List. Ford Fellowship '94-'95. Astro GPA 3.72, overall GPA 3.30.

PARKWAY NORTH SENIOR HIGH SCHOOL   *St. Louis, MO*
Class of 1991. Valedictorian, GPA 4.625 out of 4.0. National Merit Scholar. President, National Honor Society and Mu Alpha Theta. Varsity Track and Cross Country. Placed 1st in nation in National Math League, '91.

WORK EXPERIENCE

PROJECT CONSULTANT   Harvard College Observatory
Summer '93-present   *Cambridge, MA*
Developed and coded original idea for algorithm maximizing efficiency in positioning fibers of multifiber spectrograph for Professor Margaret Geller. This system will be used at the converted Multiple Mirror Telescope in Arizona. Used system to find most efficient design parameters for spectrograph being developed by Dan Fabricant.

STUDENT OBSERVER   Harvard College Observatory
Fall-Spring '94-'95   *Cambridge, MA*
Controlled operation of 1.2m radio telescope. Performed observation of CO in M31. Maintained and calibrated computer-controlled telescope. Replaced liquid helium and nitrogen. Supported data manipulation software.

TEACHING FELLOW   Harvard Engineering Sciences Department
Spring '94   *Cambridge, MA*
Led students as TF for Professor Roger Brockett's ES51: A CAD Approach to Engineering. Conducted laboratory exercises with students. Helped students understand the course material. Graded homework and tests.

COURSEWORK AND COMPUTER SKILLS

ASTROPHYSICS - PHYSICS
Radiative Processes in Modern Astrophysics, Solar System Dynamics, Galactic Structure and Dynamics, Stellar Structure and Evolution, Elementary Cosmology, Electricity and Magnetism, Special Relativity, Wave Phenomena, Quantum Mechanics, Mechanics, Statistical Mechanics and Thermodynamics, Astronomy Lab.

MATH AND RELATED STUDIES
Multivariable Calculus, Linear Algebra, Functions of Complex Variables, Linear, Ordinary and Partial Differential Equations, Calculus of Variations, Seminar on Chaos Theory, CAD Approach to Engineering, Vision and Brain.

COMPUTER KNOWLEDGE
Fluent in C, Pascal, Basic and GKS. Familiar with Fortran. Experienced with UNIX and VMS.

ACTIVITIES

HARVARD COLLEGE: Faculty-Undergraduate Concentration Committee, Professor Ramsh Narayan, *Fall '94-Spring '95,* Treasurer, ΣAM Lambda Chapter, *Sept '93-Sept '94.*

PERSONAL: Enjoy lifting weights, playing roller hockey, and rooting for the St. Louis Blues.

Comments: Because his preparation in math, physics, and astrophysics will probably be important to his potential employers, Donald Bickell has listed his courses and his computer programming skills in a separate section. Under Work Experience, he describes specific accomplishments on each job.

MARCUS BURGESS

242 Cabot Mail Center
Cambridge, MA 02138-1560
(617) 493-9546

6845 Westborough Court
Raleigh, NC 27609
(919) 482-3538

Education

HARVARD UNIVERSITY   Cambridge, MA
BA with Honors in Government expected in June 1995. Focus on international
relations and public policy. Awarded Harvard College Scholarship for academic achievement. Dean's List. 30 hr/wk year-round tennis commitment.

NEEDHAM BROUGHTON HIGH SCHOOL   Raleigh, NC
Graduated with a 4.25 GPA on a 4.0 scale. Top 4% in class of 500.
Academic All-American, junior and senior years. Captain of tennis team,
junior and senior years.

Experience

Professional Tennis Tours **UNITED STATES TENNIS ASSOCIATION**   MI, KY
Competed in the 1993 U.S. Open. Competed in a professional satellite
circuit. Summer 1994.

Fund Raiser **FRIENDS OF HARVARD TENNIS & SQUASH**   Cambridge, MA
Organized phonathon. Raised $12,000 for the Harvard Tennis and Squash
Program. Led member-guest tennis tournament. Raised $5,000 for the
Tennis Program and the Jimmy Fund. 1994-95.

Teacher **HARVARD PROGRAM FOR INTERNATIONAL EDUCATION**
Dorchester, MA
Taught international relations to an eleventh grade AP History class at
Bridgewater High School. Spring 1994. Taught U.S. relations with Latin
America to an eighth grade class at Thompson Middle School. Fall 1994.

Tennis Instructor **RALEIGH RACQUET CLUB**   Raleigh, NC
Taught beginners, ages 4-10, Summers 1990-94. Served as practice
partner/traveling mentor for national and international level players, 1992-
94. Assistant to the Director. Designed program for junior and advanced
player development, 1993-94.

Activities

Team Captain 1994-1995 **HARVARD VARSITY TENNIS TEAM**
Played #1 singles on 1994-95 IVY/ECAC Championship Team. Eastern
Region All-Star Team, 1995. Selected to compete in the Prentice Cup, one
of six players from Harvard and Yale competing against team selected from
Oxford and Cambridge, June 1995.

AMATEUR TENNIS
National Amateur Champion, 1993. North Carolina High School State
Champion, 1990-1991. Featured in *Sports Illustrated* "Faces in the Crowd,"
1991. Selected to Prince High School All-American Team, 1990-91.

Personal Working knowledge of WordPerfect, Microsoft Word, and Spanish.

Comments: Marcus Burgess has devoted most of his time, summer and winter, to
competitive tennis. Because he now wants a job in the business world, he has designed
his resume to emphasize the variety of experiences he has had within the tennis world.
He does not hide his achievement of winning the National Amateur Championship,
however, because employers in any field will respect that as a significant achievement.

Matthew Patrick Cales

524 Mather Mail Center
Cambridge, MA 02138-6175
(617) 493-6578

22 Mackenzie Street #4004
Cambridge, MA 02139
(617) 555-9043

Education

HARVARD UNIVERSITY   Cambridge, MA
Bachelor of Arts in Government (with honors) expected June 1995.
    John Harvard and Harvard College Scholarships for academic distinction. Dean's List
    all semesters. Coursework includes economics, political philosophy, Russian history,
    ancient and modern law, and Elizabethan literature.
President, Harvard Students for a Free Society; Staff writer and editor, *Harvard Salient*; Harvard
    Rugby Football Club.

STUYVESANT HIGH SCHOOL   New York, NY
Graduated with highest honors, June 1991.
    Principal's Scholar, National Merit Finalist, Webster Thierry U.S. History Award,
    Adopt-a-Child Program, Varsity Basketball.

Experience

DEAN WITTER, DISCOVER & CO.   New York, NY
Equity Division Summer Intern. Gained exposure to all aspects of equity operations,
    including: receiving reports and making inquiries for traders on institutional desk,
    reviewing financial statements of utilities for Senior Analyst report, and performing
    clerk functions on NYSE and AMEX floors. Summer 1994.

HARVARD LAW REVIEW   Cambridge, MA
Assistant to the Managing Editor. Manage coordination of research materials for leading
    law review. Reorganized and improved record-keeping system to cut research-related
    costs. Perform legal research and other related tasks. 15 hrs./wk. Fall 1993 to present.

NATIONAL TAXPAYERS UNION   Washington, DC
Legislative Analyst and Charles G. Koch Foundation Summer Fellow. Researched Senate
    franking practices to determine their effects on taxpayers and elections. Analyzed campaign
    proposals and participated in lobbying Congress. Uncovered waste and abuse in federal
    mandate system. Assembled anecdotes and wrote contributions for CEO's speeches.
    Studied debates over Balanced Budget Amendment and composed a quantitative
    analysis of positions on the issue in order to target potential supporters. Summer 1993.

HARVARD REPUBLICAN CLUB   Cambridge, MA
Vice President. Managed day-to-day activities of Harvard's oldest and largest political
    organization. Recruited over 100 new members, designed publicity system for events,
    coordinated guest speakers, and participated in public speeches and debates. Fund-
    raising effort eliminated budget deficit and created $3,000 surplus. 20 hrs./wk. 1992-93.

STACEY'S BOOKSTORE   San Francisco, CA
Assistant Bookseller. Ran 12-line phone system, took orders, handled customer inquiries,
    and managed large orders in receiving at high-volume trade bookstore. Summer 1992.

Activities and Interests

Political Campaigns: Campus Coordinator, Committee to Re-Elect Frank Duehay, Cambridge
    City Council race - 1991, 1993; Volunteer, Democratic National Committee Victory
    Fund '90; Ward Treasurer, Cambridge Republican City Committee, 1993-present.
Awards: Outstanding Young American, NTU Foundation, 1994; Student Publication Award,
    Leadership Institute, 1993; Institute for Humane Studies Fellowship recipient, 1995.
Activities: PADI certified SCUBA diver. Finisher, 1995 Boston Marathon. Enjoy
    basketball, skiing, tennis, and golf.

Comments: Matthew Cales has chosen to give greater emphasis to the employers for whom he worked than to his job titles. His rationale for listing college activities in three different sections is not clear and may dilute his message. For example, if he is applying for Republican political jobs, he could strengthen his presentation by grouping his Republican activities and the *Salient* in one section, "Political Experience."

CHARLES CESTARI

123 Winthrop Mail Center   14C Bass Circle
Cambridge, MA 02138-5724   Upper River, NY 12245
(617) 493-6625   (518) 555-2367

EDUCATION

Harvard College, Cambridge, MA. B.A. degree with honors in Social Studies expected 1995. Coursework in international development, African history, history of socialism, and social and political theory. Student Representative, Social Studies Curriculum Review Board. Harvard National Scholar (awarded to top 5 percent of entering class). John Harvard Scholarship for academic distinction. Dean's List.

Rotary Youth Exchange, Diocesan College, Cape Town, South Africa. High school cultural exchange program. Examined political and economic situations, formally and informally. (1989-90)

Worcester Central School, Worcester, NY. Student Council President. Yearbook Editor-in-Chief. Hugh O'Brian Youth Foundation, selected to represent New York at International Leadership Seminar. Semifinalist, "Jeopardy!" Teen Tournament (one of 15 contestants chosen from nearly 10,000 entrants). (1987-91)

EMPLOYMENT AND ACTIVITIES

Let's Go, Inc., Managing Editor. Recruited, hired, and managed a staff of 8 editors and 30 researcher-writers. Significant experience researching, writing, and editing. Completed final edit of over 2,400 pages of text, including *Let's Go: Europe*, the world's best-selling travel guide. Contributed to long-range plans for the organization. Served as a researcher-writer in eastern Germany for 5 weeks in summer of 1993, researching, writing, and editing chapters on Saxony and Thuringia. (1993-95)

WorldTeach, Harvard Institute for International Development, Assistant to the Director. Assist with recruitment and placement of volunteer teachers in WorldTeach's Russia Program. Train new employees. Research and prepare current news articles and social information for two 50-page educational readers. (1992-present)

Northfield Mount Hermon Summer School, Teaching Fellow. Assisted a teacher of English as a Second Language. Independently planned and taught a workshop in Word Processing and Computer Skills. Supervised recreational tennis. Served as academic and personal adviser to 20 students. (Summer 1994)

Harvard Model Congress Europe, Executive Assistant. Worked closely with 15 other students to plan and conduct a simulation of the United States Congress for European high school students. Directed publication of conference newspaper using desktop publishing techniques. (1994-95)

Harvard International Review, **Special Features Editor**. Executive Board position. Researched, solicited authors, and edited approximately one-fifth of the magazine. Directly supervised 3 to 5 research assistants. Prepared and conducted interview with Jeffrey Sachs. Authored pieces on informal economic structures in developing countries and East European nuclear technology, and book reviews on international relations theory. Also served as Special Projects Manager; participated in circulation and publicity projects and evaluated unsolicited manuscripts. (1992-94)

City of Cambridge, Assistant Registrar. Registered local residents and led registration and nonpartisan voter education campaigns. (1993-94)

RELATED SKILLS

Computer: Macintosh Microsoft Word, Microsoft Works, Excel, PageMaker, and Simply Accounting. NeXTWrite Now and Frame Maker. IBM WordPerfect and Windows.
Typing: 70 words per minute.
Travel: throughout Western Europe, North America, and Southern Africa.
Languages: fluent in English, proficient in German, Afrikaans, Dutch, and French.

Comments: Charles Cestari is interested in a position in an international organization. In planning his resume, he has mixed Employment and Activities in the center section in order to give maximum emphasis to his international experiences. The outline form of the Related Skills section communicates a lot of information efficiently.

Anna Grigg

244 Lowell Mail Center
Cambridge, MA 02138-5028
(617) 493-2997

4596 College Drive
Palo Alto, CA 94306-3801
(415) 555-9785

Education

HARVARD UNIVERSITY   Cambridge, MA
B.A. honors degree in Economics, expected June 1995. Dean's List. Elizabeth Cary Agassiz
Certificate of Merit. Currently writing an honors thesis in health care economics. Coursework
includes: the strategic management of technological innovation, applied linear regression
analysis, microeconomics, macroeconomics, multivariable calculus, linear algebra, public
finance, international trade economics, and extensive coursework in biochemistry and biology.

HENRY M. GUNN HIGH SCHOOL   Palo Alto, CA
Graduated fifth in a class of 286. National Merit Scholar. Won national awards in Future
Business Leaders of America competitions in information processing and office procedures.
Won national honors in piano performance and Latin prose and poetry. Won state awards
in biology and general sciences. Future Business Leaders of America chapter president. Peer
tutor. Youth symphony member; performed in Carnegie Hall.

Experience and College Activities

PROJECT HOPE   Washington, DC
Center for Health Affairs Intern. Worked on several ongoing projects at a major health
policy research center (Summer 1994).
- Participated in the development of the questionnaire for the Robert Wood Johnson
  Foundation's National Access to Care Survey.
- Wrote summary report for the Survey of State Regulation of Physician Office
  Equipment.
- Worked extensively with spreadsheets to perform a variety of tasks, such as:
  calculating the national distribution of Medicare benefits among races and age
  groups, calculating population changes among races and age groups, computing
  trends in the numbers of divorced women, etc.
- Consolidated project histories.
- Conducted literature searches and reviews.

PHILLIPS BROOKS HOUSE ASSOCIATION   Cambridge, MA
Co-chair of the Community Health Program. Interview and advise Harvard students
interested in health care volunteer positions: assess individual interests and capabilities, and
negotiate appropriate positions with Boston area hospitals, clinics, nursing homes, and
public health initiatives. Head student volunteers in a tri-city effort to increase immuniza-
tion rates among pre-school children. Help to coordinate public lecture series on current
health care issues (Fall 1994 to present).

NATIONAL BUREAU OF ECONOMIC RESEARCH   Cambridge, MA
Research Assistant. Provided research assistance for a working paper measuring the impact
of knowledge of a potential partner's sexual history on sexual behavior and rates of HIV
infection (Summer 1993).

HARVARD UNIVERSITY HEALTH SERVICES   Cambridge, MA
Student Health Advisory Committee Member. Served as a liaison between undergraduate
students and health services administration. Wrote newsletter article giving tips to undergraduates on how to get the best possible care from their visits to a large HMO clinic (Spring 1993).

Other Activities: Massachusetts General Hospital volunteer. Member of the Undergraduate Admissions Committee, which advises prospective freshmen. Member of the Harvard-
Radcliffe Chorus. Secretary of the Lowell House Music Society.

Computer Skills: Familiar with spreadsheet (Microsoft Excel), statistical (SAS), and word
processing (Microsoft Word, WordPerfect, Word Star) software.

Comments: Anna Grigg is seeking a position in health policy research. To
emphasize her interest and background in this field, she has devoted more space to
describing her work at Project Hope than her other jobs.

JUAN HERNANDEZ

305 Holcombe Street Apt. 5B
Cambridge, MA 02138
(617) 492-4228

460 East End Avenue Apt. 6G
New York, NY 10024
(212) 943-7677

Education

HARVARD UNIVERSITY   Cambridge, MA
B.A. in Government with a concentration in Latin America expected January 1995. Candidate for Honors. Harvard College scholar, Dean's list all semesters, Winner of One Generation After national essay competition.
- Coursework in Latin American political economy, accounting, and international relations.
- Honors thesis: **The Politics of Central Bank Autonomy in Mexico.**

BRONX HIGH SCHOOL OF SCIENCE   Bronx, NY
Graduated with Honors June 1991. National Merit semifinalist, Hispanic National Merit semifinalist, Robert C. Byrd scholar, Empire State scholar, Regents scholar.

Work Experience

Office of the President of Mexico   Mexico City, MEXICO
CONSULTANT ON NAFTA AND FOREIGN POLICY: Researched and organized President Carlos Salinas de Gortari's international speeches. Conducted policy analyses and feasibility studies. Wrote editorials and analyzed the foreign press. Also advised on NAFTA and other foreign policy issues. (March 1994 - August 1994)

Select Information Exchange   Mexico City, MEXICO
INVESTOR RELATIONS CONSULTANT: Conducted market research to locate potential Mexican companies interested in attracting U.S. investors through direct mail marketing. (June 1994 - September 1994)

Let's Go Travel   Cambridge, MA
TRAVEL CONSULTANT: Sold equipment, booked flights, and assisted customers. Top sales associate of 1993. (December 1992 - January 1994)

San Andres Hydroelectric Corporation   Cambridge, MA
TRANSLATOR: Translated from Spanish to English a several-hundred-page proposal for the sale of a State-owned hydroelectric plant in Argentina. (December 1993 - January 1994)

Radcliffe College Fund
TELEMARKETER: Raised over $10,000 in alumni outreach. (September 1992 - December 1992)

Roberta Freymann Fashion   New York, NY
PUBLIC RELATIONS LIAISON: Maintained business relations with stores, handled incoming shipments, called on accounts receivable, and assisted with bookkeeping and data entry. (September 1989 - December 1990)

Skills & Activities

Languages: Fully bilingual Spanish - English, fluency in French, conversational Italian, basic Chinese.

Computers: Knowledge of Macintosh and IBM platforms. Proficiency with Microsoft Word 5.1 and Excel 4.0.

Extracurriculars: Kennedy School of Government Projects Committee, Civics Public Service Program, Mock Trial Team, Harvard Investment Association, Harvard Organization of Latin American Students; volunteer at the Mount Sinai Hospital, tutor for a disabled girl; tennis, skiing, and intramural volleyball.

Travel: Extensive travel throughout Asia, Europe, North America, South America, and Africa, including trekking through the Amazon jungle of central Brazil, cross-country skiing in Tierra del Fuego, hitchhiking through Morocco, and studying in the People's Republic of China over the summer of 1989.

Comments: To emphasize his interest in a career in Latin America, Juan Hernandez highlights his relevant coursework and his honors thesis topic. Capitalizing the job titles instead of the employers is another way to shape the message of the resume.

REGINA A. HOLCOMB
holcomb4@husc.harvard.edu

195 Dunster Mail Center
Cambridge, MA 02138-6169
(617) 493-3488

4590 7th Avenue North
Great Falls, MT 59405
(406) 555-4365

EDUCATION

Harvard University.   Cambridge, MA
A.B. in Mathematics expected in June 1995. Additional coursework in Economics, Statistics, Physics, Chemistry, Engineering Sciences, Computer Sciences, and Music.

Great Falls High School.   Great Falls, MT
Valedictorian. National Merit Scholar. Mathematics Scholarship Award.

SKILLS

Computer Programming in Pascal, Lisp, C, and Basic; French.

WORK EXPERIENCE

Mathematics Researcher. Awarded a grant to research computer approximations of minimal surfaces at Mount Holyoke College REU (Research Experience for Undergraduates). Summer 1994.

Mathematics Course Assistant. Taught sections, tutored students, and corrected coursework for Math 21b (Linear Algebra and Differential Equations) at Harvard University. Spring term 1994.

Hotel Front Desk Assistant Manager. Supervised fellow workers, planned rooming assignments, assisted customers at Many Glacier Hotel, Glacier National Park, Montana. Summer 1993.

Grocery Store Deli Worker. Summer 1992.

Receptionist for Dan Donovan, Attorney at Law (part-time). Summer 1991.

ACTIVITIES

Orchestras (French horn).
Mozart Society Orchestra, Harvard University, 1991-1995.
Gilbert and Sullivan Players, Harvard University, 1991-1995.
Great Falls Symphony, Great Falls, Montana, 1989-1991.

Debate, both Policy and Lincoln-Douglas, for Great Falls High School team, 1987-1991.

Interests include playing piano, hiking, and skiing.

Comments: Regina Holcomb is applying for jobs as a computer programmer. To give emphasis to her skills in programming, she has placed the Skills section right after the Education section. She lists her email address on her resume because she is accessing job listings on the Internet and expects that she may apply for some jobs by email. If she sends her resume by email, she will not use boldface type.

PATRICK LAWRENCE JONES

340 Leverett Mail Center
Harvard College
Cambridge, MA 02138-6034
(617) 493-1922

Two Willow Brook Drive
He-He-Kis, NJ 07423
(201) 336-4565

EDUCATION

HARVARD COLLEGE   Cambridge, MA
B.A. in Economics expected June 1995: including coursework in securities valuation, corporate finance, econometrics, calculus, and accounting. Honors thesis analyzes behavior in collectibles prices, focusing on investment in auction market for fine paintings. Overall GPA 3.65.
John Harvard Scholarship for Academic Achievement of High Distinction
Harvard Political Review, Editor-in-Chief. Assigned and wrote articles, oversaw all editing, layout, publication, and distribution of nonpartisan quarterly magazine with circulation of 10,000, staff of 45 students.
Institute of Politics at the John F. Kennedy School of Government. Member of Student Advisory Committee, 30-member student steering committee.
JV lacrosse freshman and sophomore years.

PHILLIPS ACADEMY   Andover, MA
Graduated *cum laude* 1990; Honor Roll every term. National Merit Scholarship finalist.
Varsity tennis, JV soccer, and JV track. Worked with retarded children in after-school program.

LA SABRANAQUE   St. Victor la Coste, France
Intensive advanced French language program at village near Avignon from February to June 1991. Program included French classes and restoration of local medieval buildings.

WORK EXPERIENCE

F&S ALLOYS AND MINERALS CORPORATION, Sales Assistant New York, NY
F&S Alloys, a subsidiary of the German corporation Stinnes, is a worldwide leader in trading industrial metals, minerals, chemicals, and other products.
• Identified and solicited potential corporate clients for commodities sales.
• Produced market surveys and project evaluations for foreign firms seeking to enter the North American market.
• Created and implemented a marketing strategy for selling silica fume from Eastern European producer to American firms, presented findings to client management.
• Provided technical analysis of futures prices for commodities traded on London Metal Exchange, and advised traders accordingly. Summers 1993, 1994.

EAST HARLEM FAMILY CENTER, Volunteer Social Worker   New York, NY
Consulted with homeless families daily regarding welfare, medical, legal, and immigration issues. Managed four cases; relocated 2 families to permanent housing and assisted in relocation of 15 additional families. Tracked progress of families in after-care programs. September 1990 - January 1991.

DEVON YACHT CLUB, Head Counselor   Amagansett, NY
Supervised approximately 30 children aged 6-9. Organized field trips, developed and taught daily activities program including sailing, swimming, and tennis. Summers 1990, 1991, 1992.

COMPUTER SKILLS: Lotus 1-2-3, Excel, TSP, WordPerfect, Microsoft Word
INTERESTS: Tennis, golf, skiing, running, sailing, politics
TRAVEL: Traveled extensively throughout Western Europe

Comments: To highlight his qualifications for jobs in investment banking and management consulting, Patrick Jones lists his relevant coursework and thesis topic in the first paragraph and uses bullets to emphasize his various accomplishments in two summers at F&S Alloys.

Robert Joseph Mattix

433 Mather Mail Center
Harvard College
Cambridge, MA 02138-6175
(617) 493-6547

Permanent Address:
17 Rodeo Road
Irvine, CA 92720
(714) 558-9857

Education

HARVARD UNIVERSITY   Cambridge, MA
A.B. Honors degree in Government expected 1995. Dean's list. Coursework in
International Political Economics and the European Community. Commit 25 hours per
week to the Harvard Varsity Football Program. Worked 5 to 15 hours per week term-
time to defray cost of tuition.

INSTITUTE FOR THE STUDY OF ECONOMICS AND POLITICS   London, England
Studied the Government and Political Economics of Europe through Butler University
and the London School of Economics. January-April 1993.

PHILLIPS EXETER ACADEMY   Exeter, NH
Graduated *cum laude* in 1990. Member of Varsity Football Program.

Business Experience

THE HAMMOND COMPANY, THE MORTGAGE BANKERS   Newport Beach, CA
Worked in Loan Origination and Quality Control auditing and insuring funded loan files
and as Management Intern to the Executive Vice President of Corporate Operations.
Initiated, organized, and implemented fundamental changes in back room operations.
Worked 50 to 80 hours per week while on voluntary one-semester leave of absence from
Harvard College, June-January 1994-1995.

MERRILL LYNCH, PIERCE, FENNER & SMITH LIMITED   London, England
Interned in Equities Research for the European Investment Strategy Director. Together with
Assistant Vice President, produced a spreadsheet for graphing and evaluating sector
performance in Europe. Worked 24 hours per week, January-April 1993.

THOMAS WILCK ASSOCIATES   Newport Beach, CA
Assistant Account Executive. A medium-sized public relations and communications firm.
Researched and assembled requests for proposals. Actively participated in staff meetings and
brainstorming sessions. Generated correspondence with top executive officers. Summer 1992.

ALEX. BROWN & SONS INC.   Baltimore, MD
Industry Orientation Internship. Participated in explanatory one-on-one discussions with
professionals in various departments including mutual funds, corporate finance, trading,
municipals, capital management, mergers and acquisitions, and retail brokerage. Spring
Break 1992.

COLDWELL BANKER   Laguna Hills, CA
Implemented new computer system. Input and reorganized client information. Used
newly initiated program to simplify formulation of client mailing lists and incorporate
currently filed information. December-January 1991-1992.

Skills & Activities

Computer Skills: Worked with major computer software programs, including MS
Word, WordPerfect, MS Excel, MS Powerpoint, MS Publisher, MS Money, and Borland
Quattro Pro and Paradox.

Currently working towards California Real Estate License by correspondence through
The Real Estate Trainers.

Traveled extensively in Europe alone (May-August 1993). Enjoy running, skiing, and
mountain biking.

Comments: To explain his lack of college activities, Robert Mattix lists his
participation in Varsity Football and part-time work commitment in the first paragraph. To emphasize his experience in banking, he uses bold capitals for the names
of his employers and even includes his spring break internship at Alex. Brown & Sons.

JASON NEIL

353 Leverett Mail Center
Cambridge, MA 02138-6034
617/493-3756

84 E. Houseman Street
Westerville, OH 43081
614/782-0642

Education

HARVARD UNIVERSITY   Cambridge, MA
A.B. in Chemistry and Physics expected in June 1995. Honors candidate. Additional coursework in economics, mathematics, and dramatic arts.

WESTERVILLE SOUTH   Westerville, OH
National Merit Scholar, Class President, Varsity Cross Country, Student Council, Drama, Marching Band (trumpet), Jazz Band, Mock Trial, Youth-to-Youth drug prevention program.

Activities

HASTY PUDDING THEATRICALS   Harvard University
President. Coordinate efforts of outside creative, musical, and technical professionals. Manage company of 60 undergraduates in annual $300,000 production. April 1994-Present. *Cast*: Acted in student-written musicals, with annual runs of 43 performances each. December 1991-Present.

LEVERETT HOUSE ARTS SOCIETY   Harvard University
Drama President. House Theater Coordinator. Secured talent and doubled number of theater productions. Directed two full-length plays. Acted in two productions. Converted unused basement space into experimental theater. September 1992-Present.

Work and Research Experience

HARVARD BUSINESS SCHOOL   Cambridge, MA
Dictated case studies for blind student. Gained exposure and understanding of venture capital, market forces, and corporate analysis. Fall 1994.

HARVARD DEPT. OF EARTH AND PLANETARY SCIENCES   Cambridge, MA
Analyzed oxidation states of ancient earth soils to determine prehistoric atmospheric composition. Developed literature search skills. Independent work culminated in research paper. Spring 1994.

ASHLAND CHEMICAL, INC.   Dublin, OH
Developed proficiency in project and time management and data analysis. *Foundry Products Division:* Synthesis and materials testing of phenolic binder resins. *Analytical Section:* Determination and quantification of competitor product composition using HPLC and GC. *Industrial Hygiene:* Determination of pollution levels by GC for industrial monitoring program. Summers 1992-1994.

COLUMBUS DISPATCH   Columbus, OH
Delivered daily paper. 65 customers. Doubled number of subscribers. Named top carrier out of 50,000 in state. Enhanced skills in customer service. 1986-1991.

RELEVANT SKILLS: Public speaking, Microsoft Word, Excel, WordPerfect.

INTERESTS: Acting, Taekwondo, singing, travel, psychology, and personal investing.

Comments: Jason Neil gives emphasis to his experience and leadership in theater productions by placing Activities as the second section, above Work and Research Experience. This reinforces the message that he wants employment in the theater or the arts rather than the sciences.

LISA SEINFELD

211 Currier Mail Center
Cambridge, MA 02138-1598
(617) 493-7800

78 Stanford Circle
Madison, NJ 07940
(201) 555-0045

EDUCATION

Harvard University - A.B. in Social Anthropology expected in June, 1995.
Honors candidate, thesis on **Routenization of Charisma in the Hawkins Dance Company**. Additional coursework in philosophy, economics, and math. Recipient of:

Ford Foundation Grant and **Goelet Fund Grant** for thesis research with
Erick Hawkins Dance Company, Summer 1994.

Louise Green Bursley Travelling Fellowship awarded by Radcliffe
College, to fund teaching and research in Latvia, Summer 1993.

Madison High School - 1991 Salutatorian; Presidential Scholar; Perfect score on
S.A.T. (1600); National Merit Scholar; Yearbook Editor-in-Chief.

WORK EXPERIENCE

Producer of the Dunster House Opera Society. Coordinated and supervised 100
students in a full-scale production of "Die Fledermaus." School year 1994-95.

Course Assistant for *General Education 156: The Information Age*, also offered as
a Kennedy School of Government course. Graded papers, exams; stimulated
class discussion. School year 1994-95.

Intern to Executive Director of the Erick Hawkins Dance Company. Wrote grant
proposals, National Association of Schools of Dance accreditation application;
registered copyrights, etc. Summer 1994.

Curriculum Developer and English Teacher at a hospital in Bauska, Latvia. 2-
month program offered to 40 students. Summer 1993.

Tutor for Harvard Bureau of Study Counsel in anthropology, philosophy, and
economics, school years 1993-1995; privately and on a volunteer basis for National
Honor Society in math, English, science, French, and composition, 1991-1993.

Summer work experience as: Playground Supervisor; Temporary Clerical Worker;
Daytime Caretaker; Bookkeeper, Receptionist, and Assistant in a dentist's office;
Cashier and Waitress.

ACTIVITIES

Producer 1994; **Title Role in "Carmen"** 1994 - Dunster House Opera Society.

Choreographer and **Performer** - Mainly Jazz Dance Company, 1992-present.

Member - Harvard/Radcliffe Collegium Musicum, 1993-1995.

Lead Roles, Choreographer, Dance Captain - college, community, and high
school musical theater.

ADDITIONAL SKILLS

Computer - Word processing, Excel, some familiarity with NEXIS.
Arts - Piano, cello, crocheting.

Comments: Lisa Seinfeld is seeking employment in public relations or advertising.
Her resume documents her experiences in the performing arts which makes clear
that she is a very creative person, but also has organizational and teaching skills.

CAROL SOZAKA

499 Kirkland Mail Center
95 Dunster Street
Cambridge, MA 02138-5912
(617) 493-3698

66 Wedgewood Road
Providence, RI 02906
(401) 532-1184

EDUCATION

Harvard University   **Cambridge, MA**
A.B. with honors degree in Biochemical Sciences, expected in June 1995. Elizabeth
Cary Agassiz Certificate of Merit for academic achievement of high distinction. Wood
Memorial Scholarship. Dean's List. Electives in Japanese history, psychology, creative
writing, and dramatic arts.

Classical High School   **Providence, RI**
Valedictorian of the class of 1991. Graduated *summa cum laude*. National Merit
Scholarship; Rhode Island Governor's Academic Scholarship; Rhode Island Distin-
guished Merit Senior in Math, Science, and English; Rensellaer Medal recipient;
Providence College Chemistry Award.

WORK EXPERIENCE

Summer Intern
Rhode Island Department of Health, Division of Family Health   **Providence, RI**
Compiled and organized information to set up a physician referral service. Researched and
summarized information about Medicaid Managed Care. Assisted with phone surveys of
community health centers. Designed forms for prenatal care program. Summer 1994.

Lab Assistant
Dana Farber Cancer Institute, Division of Tumor Immunology   **Boston, MA**
Conducted lab research of the oncogene *lck* in T lymphocytes. Summer 1993 and Spring
1994.

Office Assistant
Graduate Student Council, Harvard University   **Cambridge, MA**
Managed office and computer room. Organized files. Fall 1992 through Spring 1993.

Lab Assistant
Rhode Island Department of Health, Diagnostic Microbiology Lab   **Providence, RI**
Managed strep throat cultures and various lab procedures. Summer 1992.

Advertising Sales Representative
Harvard Student Agencies   **Cambridge, MA**
Sold advertising space in *The Unofficial Guide to Life at Harvard* to local store owners
and national chains. Achieved a complete sellout of advertising space. Spring and
Summer 1992.

Research Assistant
The Miriam Hospital, Department of Behavioral Medicine   **Providence, RI**
Conducted statistical analysis of data for study determining the effects of personality on
heart risk factors and summarized results of analysis. Summer 1991.

ACTIVITIES

House Coordinator and Tutor for the Harvard House and Neighborhood Development
Program (HAND), which plans public service and community action programs in an
effort to stimulate interaction between college students and Cambridge neighborhoods.
Hospital Volunteer at the Massachusetts General Hospital and the Children's Hospital.
Tutor for the Inner City Outreach Program, Phillips Brooks House, Harvard University.
Ballet with the Radcliffe Dance Program.

Comments: Carol Sozaka has deferred her acceptance to medical school and is
seeking a job in a medical setting. Because she wants an opportunity to interact with
patients, she has described her various tutoring experiences under Activities.

JOSEPH DAVID SALERNO
23 Linear Street, No. 4
Somerville, MA 02143
(617) 767-7447

Education

HARVARD UNIVERSITY   Cambridge, MA
A.B. *cum laude* in Government, February 1993. Harvard College Scholarship for academic achievement. Dean's List. Ran several term-time businesses to pay tuition. Financially independent since 1988.

OTAGO UNIVERSITY   Dunedin, New Zealand
Rotary International Ambassadorial Scholarship: researched Maori/Pakeha race relations in New Zealand. Spoke to Rotary Clubs and high schools throughout New Zealand about racial politics. February-December 1994.

Work Experience

Assistant Managing Director **UNIVERSITY SEMINARS**   Cambridge, MA
Planned and implemented all aspects of international executive education conferences designed for senior East Asian business executives. Co-developed curriculum. Hired university professors. Designed company brochures and advertising. Coordinated international marketing program. Arranged conference, language, protocol, and entertainment logistics. Initiated expansion into Pakistan, Singapore, Hong Kong, and Malaysia. Maintained financial and tax records. Hired and trained employees. February 1993-February 1994.

Teaching Fellow **HARVARD UNIVERSITY**   Cambridge, MA
Designed and led weekly tutorial for Dr. Robert Coles' course, "The Literature of Social Reflection." Awarded the *Harvard University Certificate of Distinction in Teaching*, based on anonymous student evaluations (*The CUE Guide*). Received highest rating of any teaching fellow at Harvard College during the fall semester of 1993.

Computer Salesperson **SALERNO ELECTRONICS**   Denver, CO
Sold $80,000 of computer equipment in 3 months. Wrote, designed, and published *PC Quarterly Newsletter* and an introductory MS-DOS manual, both aimed at repositioning the company as a Value Added Retailer. Assisted with market research and technical support. Summers, 1990 and 1992.

Research Associate **HARVARD UNIVERSITY DEVELOPMENT OFFICE**   Cambridge, MA
Researched prospective major donors. Assisted gift officers in determination of alumni contribution levels. Worked 20 additional hours each week with New Boston Group soliciting Harvard alumni donations by phone. Summer, 1991.

Front-Desk Clerk **IMPERIAL HAWAII RESORT**   Honolulu, HI
Handled reservations, check-in, and irate travelers. Trained new employees and advised general manager on computer purchases. Winter/Spring, 1990.

Activities and Interests

Business Editor, *The Harvard Crimson*, 1990-92.
Group Leader, First-Year Outdoor Program, 1990-92.
Counselor, Room 13 Peer Counseling, 1991-93.
Committee Member, Harvard Foundation Student Advisory Committee on Race Relations, 1991-92.
Cited for *Outstanding Contributions to Inter-Cultural Life at the University.*
Committee Member, 1993 Class Committee. Founder of the Michael Berry award.
Full-Back, Harvard Rugby Team, 1991-92.
Pitcher, Harvard Baseball Team, 1990-91.
Manager, Harvard Women's Swim Team, 1991-92.
Rock Climbing, Jazz Saxophone, Mountain Biking.

Comments: Joseph Salerno graduated two years ago and has just returned from a year in New Zealand. By using bold for the position titles on his list of college activities, he highlights his leadership experience. Placing job titles in the left margin emphasizes the diversity of his work experiences.

Peter D. Cleck

16 Chatham Street
Arlington, MA 02174
617/ 646-3860

Harvard University
Department of Physics
Cambridge, MA 02138
617/495-0408

EDUCATION

Harvard University, Ph.D., Physics, expected 1996. **M.A.**, Physics, 1993.
National Science Foundation Fellow, Condensed Matter Theory.
Freedman Fellowship for outstanding achievement in graduate school (1992).
Business Management Study Group, Harvard University (Fall 1994).
Finance Theory in Continuous Time, Audit, Professor R. Merton, Harvard
Business School (Fall 1994).
Northwestern University, M. Music, Cello performance, 1991. Fellowship student.
Princeton University, A.B., *magna cum laude*, Physics, 1990. Honors: Phi Beta Kappa, Sigma Xi.
Winner: National Merit, Jones, and Edmonds Scholarships.

RESEARCH

Doctoral thesis in Condensed Matter Theory, Harvard University (in progress).
Senior thesis on physics of the early universe, Princeton University (1989-1990).
Research position in theoretical atomic physics, Rice University (Summer 1989).
Designed, wrote, and installed software for ongoing computations in atomic physics.

TEACHING

Harvard University Teaching Fellow. Taught physics to both science and humanities
concentrators (1993-1995).
Harvard Summer Teaching Fellow. Taught physics daily to a class with little math
background (1994).
Princeton University Tutor. Tutored students one-on-one (1989-1990).

BUSINESS

Notis Systems, Illinois. Edited technical documents and performed clerical duties (1990-91).
LeBair Financial Services, Houston, Texas. Designed systems for client financial reporting
(Summers 1987, 1988).

MUSICAL

Freelance cellist in the Houston, Boston, and New York areas (1985-1993). Member of the
Princeton String Quartet (1988-1990). Solo, Chamber, and Orchestral performance in the
U.S. and Canada, including Boston, Toronto, Montreal, and Houston; **solo appearances**
with the Houston Youth Symphony, and **broadcast performance** with the Corpus Christi
Symphony (as the winner of an international competition); participation in internationally
acclaimed festivals, including Tanglewood, Aspen, and the International Congress of
Strings; **Principal cellist** of the Princeton University Orchestra, Texas All-State Orchestra,
and Houston Youth Symphony. **Grand Prize**, Corpus Christi Young Artists Competition
(1985). **Chairman,** Membership, Princeton University Orchestra (1989-1990).

VOLUNTEER

St. James Shelter, Somerville, Massachusetts. Worked mornings in a long-term shelter
designed to help people find employment and housing (Summer 1994).

SKILLS & INTERESTS

Computer skills: Programming experience in FORTRAN, APL, BASIC, and DBASEIII.
Language ability: French.
Interests: Economics, Cello pedagogy, Jogging, Backpacking, and the Outdoors.

Comments: To highlight his interest in a career in finance, Peter Cleck has listed
his two courses related to business and finance in the first section. He has also sorted
out his business experience into a separate section and he can discuss each of these
exposures to finance more fully in his cover letters.

SUZANNE M. LILLY
103 Commonwealth Avenue
Boston, MA 02122
H - (617) 555-1234   W - (617) 555-5678

EDUCATION

HARVARD UNIVERSITY Ph.D. expected October 1995 in Biology.
Dissertation on the dynamics of Eskimo hunting in a multi-prey system.
Mathematical models and multivariate statistical techniques are used
to examine causes of variation in harvest levels of wildlife populations.

M.SC. in Zoology, University of British Columbia, 1986.
Thesis on population dynamics of marmots.

B.SC. in Biology (Honors), University of Victoria, Canada, 1981.

PROFESSIONAL EXPERIENCE

STATISTICAL CONSULTANT, Marttila and Kiley, Boston. April-
May 1994.
Recommended statistical techniques for analysis of political polls.

**TEACHING FELLOW, Harvard University and University of
British Columbia Biology Departments.** 1993.

DIRECTOR OF RESEARCH, Baffin Region Inuit Association,
Northwest Territories, Canada. 1987-1992.
Designed and managed the first successful survey of wildlife harvest levels
in the Northwest Territories. Raised over $1,000,000 to fund the project.
Through public meetings, persuaded 99% of Eskimo hunters in the eastern
Arctic to participate in the survey. Managed budget and designed
accounting system. Hired and supervised a staff of 20. Statistically
analyzed a 3-million-piece data set using custom computer programs.

**PROJECT MANAGER, Consultant to Northwest Territories
Wildlife Service.** 1986-1987.
Assessed the impact of construction of a highway on wildlife populations. First in N.W.T. to implement a statistical model to estimate
numbers of moose not observed during aerial surveys.

WILDLIFE BIOLOGIST, Northwest Territories Wildlife Service.
1985-1986.
Conducted research on population dynamics of polar bears, caribou,
seals, and falcons. Authored reports with management recommendations.

SKILLS

Analytical ability: Accounting, computer programming, and statistics.
Developed a system for predicting point spread in National Football
League games. Scored in top 1% in Graduate Record Exam.
Language training: Spanish, French, Latin, Inukitut (Eskimo)
Communication skills: scientific papers, successful funding
proposals, political analyst for CBC radio

CITIZENSHIP: Dual U.S.-Canadian

Comments: Suzanne is applying for positions in investment banking. She has
planned her resume to communicate her familiarity with statistical analysis. She
describes her administrative and supervisory experience as Director of Research,
and communicates an adventurous spirit and breadth of interests. Her dual
citizenship is important information for a potential employer.

WRITING LETTERS

You may not have had much experience in writing letters. If not, now is a good time to develop this very important skill. In your ongoing career development, the letters that you write can be as important as your resume.

Letters provide the opportunity to communicate your message in a personal, yet professional way. Avoid using a form letter. Tailor each letter to the person to whom it is addressed. Before you write a letter, think about the person you are writing to and what you want to communicate to him.

The types of letters that you will be writing in the process of managing your career include the following: letters requesting a career advisory interview, letters inquiring about employment opportunities, letters applying for a job, thank-you letters, letters accepting a job, letters declining a job offer or withdrawing from a competition, and follow-up letters to any of the above.

The letters you write to career advisers and employers are an opportunity to present yourself and to initiate or reinforce a relationship. In career exploration and job-hunting letters, your objective is to motivate the recipient to invite you for an interview. In thank-you letters, your objective is to express your appreciation, add information omitted in the interview, and express interest in a continuing relationship. In a letter accepting a job, you want to accept enthusiastically and confirm the terms of your employment. In a letter declining a job offer or withdrawing, your objective is to express your appreciation and tell the employer that you have accepted another offer.

A follow-up letter can come after any of the above types of letters. It is written to reinforce the first letter, add new information, request reconsideration, or report on progress.

Letters are personal communications from you to another individual. Within the constraints of expected form and style, you should express your individuality. The appearance, form, style, and content of the letter all contribute to the messages you convey and influence the evaluation and response of the reader.

Appearance. Each letter should be addressed to an individual, printed or typed on plain paper with a matching envelope. If you are enclosing a resume, the letter and resume should be done on matching bond paper. Most business correspondence is done on white paper with black type, but ecru paper is acceptable. If you have a choice of fonts, it is recommended that you use 10-12 point type. Anything smaller than 10 point type is too difficult to read.

Letters should have absolutely no errors: no typos, no misspelled words, no grammatical errors. Take time to edit your letter. If your word processing program has a spell check, be sure you use it, but remember that you still have to proofread to catch misspellings of sound-alike words such as "their/there," or "capital/capitol," etc. Remember that every letter you send is a sample of your writing ability.

Form. Each letter should be short, fitting easily on one page with generous margins of at least one inch on all sides. Paragraphs should be limited to four to eight lines whenever possible, because employment letters are usually scanned quickly. The first line of each paragraph should state the message of that paragraph. As you rework drafts of letters, try reading only the first lines of each paragraph to see what information is conveyed in a quick scan.

Standard business form, with your address and the date at the top and the addressee's name and address at the left just above the salutation, is preferable. Your full name may be typed below your signature at the end of the letter or at the top with the address. Remember to sign your letters and make copies for your files.

Letters should be addressed to an individual by name, with his correct title and address. If you do not know the person's title, call the company and ask for the correct title. Titles should be used in the salutation, if appropriate, such as "Dear Dr. Carley" or "Dear Judge O'Neil," but in most correspondence the salutation will be "Dear Mr. Smith" or "Dear Ms. White." First names should not be used unless you are personally acquainted with the addressee. It is advisable to try to find out whether a woman prefers to be addressed as "Miss," "Mrs.," or "Ms.," but if her preference is not known, "Ms." is acceptable.

Style. Your letters should express individuality and personality and communicate that you would "fit in" to the organization. To show respect for the reader's time, you want to be forthright, informative, and concise. Employment letters are not supposed to have the flow of literary prose, but should be written to communicate information with clarity and impact. Simple direct sentences are usually preferable. Within these constraints, there is a great deal of latitude for personal choice of words and sentence structure.

The following descriptions and sample letters are meant to provide helpful suggestions and models.

Career Exploration Letters

A letter requesting an interview for career advice should engage the interest of the reader in you and your quest for information about his career field. You are asking a busy person to spend a little time discussing his work experiences and his perspectives on career opportunities. Therefore, your letter should give enough information about you and about why you selected the addressee as a potential career adviser to make him want to meet with you.

In the first paragraph, it is usual to identify yourself and request an opportunity to meet. If you were referred to the person by a mutual friend, you should mention the friend's name in the first sentence. If you obtained his name in another way, mention how you selected him as a potential career adviser. Try to limit the first paragraph to three or four lines.

In one of the middle paragraphs, describe your interest in that career field and what you would like to learn in this information interview. You might make reference to some related reading you have done. In this paragraph you want to make clear why this person can be particularly helpful to you in your career search.

In another paragraph, you should talk about yourself. This paragraph should highlight and expand upon selected relevant experiences that are listed on your resume. If you are not enclosing a resume, use this paragraph to present a brief introduction to your experiences. However, you will usually want to enclose a resume because it is such an efficient way to communicate your background.

The closing paragraph should clarify your next step. Usually it is best to state when you will be available for an interview and that you will call to arrange a mutually convenient time. This way you save the career adviser the time and expense of writing you a letter. If the career adviser is far away, however, you may have to rely on his responding by mail.

Employment Inquiry Letters

When you identify a type of job that interests you or hear about an organization for which you would like to work, you will want to seek the opportunity to meet someone in the organization. You may want to have your first meeting with someone in a position similar to what you would be seeking, but when you have gathered some information about the organization, you will want to meet with the top executive of the organization or with the department head who has the power to hire you.

This letter is similar to a career exploration letter in that you are requesting advice and not applying for employment, but now you are seeking job-hunting advice and very specific information about entry-level jobs and career pathways in that organization or similar organizations. The introductory sentence should arouse the reader's interest in you. If you have a personal referral or any kind of link with the potential employer, be sure that you state it prominently.

In the middle paragraphs, you should demonstrate that you have researched the company and the industry, perhaps by mentioning some recent reference in the news. In a separate paragraph, highlight and expand on information in your resume that is particularly relevant to this career field. Make clear why you think you are well qualified for this type of work.

In the closing paragraph, express your interest in seeking advice from this person, and state that you will call at some specific time in the near future, usually in about a week, to arrange a mutually convenient time for an interview. You are writing to a busy executive; save him the time and expense of responding by letter.

Job Application Letters

Never send a resume alone when applying for a job. Whether you hear about the job opening from a friend, read about it in the newspaper or a magazine, or find it in campus job listings, learn as much as you can about the employer and the job and use this knowledge when you are preparing your cover letter.

The objective of the cover letter is to impress the employer with your qualifications, motivation, and interest in the job so that he will want to interview you. The first paragraph should identify clearly what job you are applying for, how you learned about the opening, and why you are interested. If a mutual friend recommended that you apply for the job, mention his name.

In the middle paragraphs, discuss your qualifications for the job and your interest in the organization.

- Expand on selected accomplishments listed on your resume to illustrate relevant skills and work characteristics that you bring to the job.
- Do not make evaluative statements, such as, "I believe that I am an outstanding candidate for this position" or "I am superbly qualified for this position." It is your role to present your qualifications; it is the employer's role to evaluate them.
- Communicate your interest in the organization by expressing enthusiasm for their product line or services, or by mentioning some recent news item related to the organization or industry that impressed you. If you don't know enough about the organization to comment, express your interest in the industry.

How you divide this into two or three paragraphs will depend on your messages and what you want to emphasize. Sometimes a paragraph on relevant work experience and one on academic experience makes sense. Remember, your lead sentences should state important information succinctly and your paragraphs should be only four to eight lines long.

In the closing paragraph, express your interest in meeting with the employer to discuss the requirements of the job and your qualifications.

If you have not heard from the employer within a reasonable amount of time (perhaps a week or two), telephone the individual to whom you addressed your letter to find out how the job search is progressing. Ask if there is any further information they would like you to provide. This will give you the opportunity to communicate your continued interest in the position and may lead to an interview.

Thank-You Letters

You should write a thank-you letter to everyone with whom you meet as promptly as possible. Your thank-you letter after a job interview should be mailed or delivered within 24 hours after your interview. Even if the interviewer wasn't helpful or you are no longer interested in the job, it is important to thank the person for the time he spent with you.

The purpose of your thank-you letter after a career advising interview is to express appreciation, build goodwill, and reinforce your relationship. You might discuss briefly how the interview was helpful to you, or recount further reflections you have had on questions which were discussed. If the person gave you names to contact, thank him and let him know when you will be contacting those people. If the person gave you specific suggestions or advice on your job hunt, tell him how you plan to implement them. Do not delay your thank-you letter until you have taken action on the adviser's advice or referrals. Plan to write again when you have follow-up to report. Be sure you express your appreciation for his time and assistance. If you want to stay in contact with the person, say that you will write or call when you have progress to report.

The purpose of the thank-you letter after a job interview is to express appreciation, restate your interest in the position, and reinforce your qualifications for the job. The first paragraph should express your enthusiasm about the job and appreciation for the interview. The middle paragraph should restate your qualifications for the job. Incorporating information you learned during the interview, you might highlight your special strengths as an applicant. The last paragraph should restate your enthusiasm and willingness to supply any information that might be helpful to the employer.

If you have multiple interviews for one position during a full- or half-day visit, it is not necessary to write to everyone with whom you spoke. Instead, write to the person who arranged your visit and ask him to convey your thanks to the others with whom you met. If one of the people with whom you interviewed would be your supervisor, it is appropriate to write to him as well.

Thank-you letters can make you stand out because so few people write them. They should be short, substantive, friendly, and prompt. If your handwriting is very legible, you may send handwritten thank-you notes.

Letters of Acceptance

Although a job offer is often communicated in person or by telephone, you should expect a follow-up letter confirming the terms of employment (salary, benefits, starting date, medical examinations, etc.). You should accept the job offer in writing.

In the first paragraph you should confirm your acceptance and express your enthusiasm for joining the organization. In the middle paragraph you should confirm logistics such as when you will report to work and the requirements, if any, that you will take care of before that time. The concluding paragraph should express your appreciation for the opportunity and reiterate that you are happy to be joining their staff.

This letter can be brief and upbeat, but it should be professional in tone and format.

Withdrawal Letters

Once you accept a position, you have the ethical obligation to inform other employers of your decision and to withdraw your employment applications. Your letter should express appreciation for the employers' consideration and attention. It is appropriate to tell them what position you have accepted, but do not say that it is a better job! There is no need to alienate these other employers. You might be interested in working for any one of them at a later time in your career.

If you decide to decline a job offer that you have received, do so by letter as soon as you have made your decision. In writing a letter declining an offer, you want to express your appreciation for the offer and the confidence in your abilities that it indicates. Your objective is to reject the offer, but maintain a relationship with the employer. Be sure that you thank the employer for the offer and for his consideration of you as a candidate.

Follow-Up Letters

There are a variety of circumstances during a job search when you might want to write a follow-up letter:

- to reinforce the first letter of any type, if you have not received any response
- to add new information to an employment application
- to request reconsideration after being rejected for an job interview
- to communicate continued interest in a job or in being interviewed when the search process is protracted

• to report progress—for example, to update a member of your network or to report to an adviser on action taken on his advice or referrals

Every person with whom you have interviews while you are exploring careers or job hunting may become a friend, adviser, or mentor if you keep in touch. The initiative for continuing the relationship should come from you. If you have a career information interview that is productive and enjoyable, you should not only send an immediate thank-you note, but also write additional brief letters when you have some progress to report.

When you have accepted a job, you should share your good news by writing a brief note to all the people who assisted you in your career exploration and job hunting. Maintaining contact with people in a variety of companies or organizations is important for your ongoing career network.

The following sample letters and comments illustrate some of the principles of letter writing. They should help you to formulate your requests for career advice and to conduct an effective job search.

Career Exploration Letter 1

621 Quincy Mail Center
Cambridge, MA 02138-6609
February 28, 1995

Mr. John Roden
Vice President
Smith and O'Hare, Inc.
83 Park Avenue
New York, NY 10021

Dear Mr. Roden:

Would it be possible to meet with you to discuss careers in public relations when I am visiting in New York next month during spring vacation? I am seeking information about what public relations firms do and how a liberal arts graduate can qualify for employment in the field.

I am a junior at Harvard majoring in philosophy. A career that demands creativity and involves writing is very exciting to me. In my extracurricular activities, I usually assume the responsibility for publicity. I enjoy thinking of ways to publicize events: making posters, writing ads for the newspaper, and thinking up new gimmicks to attract attention to a specific event.

I will call you next week in hope of arranging to meet with you in your office on Thursday, March 30, or Friday, March 31.

Sincerely,

Deborah Kent

Comments: In this direct and explicit letter, Deborah shows she has given some thought to the characteristics and skills required for public relations.

Career Exploration Letter 2

35 Irving Street
Cambridge, MA 02138
November 5, 1994

Mr. Norman Walters
Commercial Lending Officer
Chemical Bank
315 Wall Street
New York, NY 10172

Dear Mr. Walters:

I have just completed my Ph.D. in English and am interested in learning about careers in commercial banking. I selected your name from the Career Advisory File because you earned a Ph.D. in history.

I have an appointment this year as an instructor in expository writing, but I am devoting as much time as I can to exploring nonacademic careers.

Banking is a career option that I have been reading and thinking about for some time. I would like to visit you at Chemical Bank to talk about your work. Your impressions of the challenges and satisfactions of your banking career as compared with those found in an academic career would be of great interest to me. In addition, I would like to learn more about the ways in which your graduate training prepared you for your career in banking.

I will call you next week to see if I can arrange a mutually convenient time to meet with you on November 15 or 16, when I will be in New York.

Sincerely,

William Clark

Comments: Although this lead sentence might not be appropriate in a letter to a non-Ph.D., in this case it identifies a common history with Mr. Walters, who has been in banking for only two years. William makes explicit that, by taking an appointment as an instructor, he has arranged time for his career exploration and job hunt.

Career Exploration Letter 3

192 Currier Mail Center
Cambridge, MA 02138-1598
May 3, 1995

Ms. Doreen Snyder
Research Director
Foreign Policy Institute
1300 Pennsylvania Avenue
Washington, DC 20006

Dear Ms. Snyder:

I read with interest your article on Southeast Asia in the last issue of *Foreign Policy*, and would like to have the opportunity to meet with you to discuss careers in international relations.

Currently, I am a junior at Harvard concentrating in government. For my senior honors thesis, I am conducting a study of United States policy toward Vietnam during the 1950s.

I have a strong interest in working in international relations and would like to discuss with you the career opportunities and entry-level jobs in the field. Your advice on graduate study would also be greatly appreciated.

I will be in Washington during June to research some primary source materials for my thesis. I will call you when I arrive to see if there is a convenient time when I might come to talk with you.

Sincerely,

George Coulter

Comments: Doreen Snyder is not a career adviser, so George states in the first paragraph how he identified her. Mention of his senior thesis topic identifies an area of shared interest and indicates he is developing a background in foreign policy research.

Career Exploration Letter 4

26 Winthrop Street
Cambridge, MA 02138
July 5, 1995

Mr. Clarence Duggan
Vice President of Marketing
McArdle Industries
101 Princeton Street
Philadelphia, PA 19105

Dear Mr. Duggan:

Mr. Malcolm Battle suggested that I write to you because of my interest in learning about the consumer products industry and most especially about the marketing of consumer products.

From my reading and from conversation with Mr. Battle, I have become excited about the data analysis and creative planning that go into developing marketing strategy. It sounds challenging and fascinating to me.

I have a strong quantitative background from academic work in sociology. I have done several projects that require compilation and analysis of demographic data. Now I am looking for opportunities to apply these skills in business.

I will be in Philadelphia at the end of July and will call next week to see if I may visit you to talk about careers in marketing.

Sincerely,

Martha Sullivan

Comments: Martha decided not to mention in this letter that she has completed a Ph.D., but she will discuss that with Mr. Duggan during the interview. She indicates that she has some knowledge of marketing already, which should make a positive impression on Mr. Duggan.

Employment Inquiry Letter 1

5104 Crawford, N.W.
Washington, DC 20008
February 25, 1995

Ms. Joan Meyer
Principal
Washington Cathedral Elementary School
3500 Crowley Road, N.W.
Washington, DC 20016

Dear Ms. Meyer:

Writing and biology became my academic loves in high school, and they remain my strongest academic interests today. Now, as a Harvard graduate, I seek the chance to teach writing and biology.

I enjoy young people. I feel comfortable with the subjects I hope to teach. I work with energy and enthusiasm, patience and persistence. Through my work with college students and young children, I have learned how to listen, how to encourage learning, and how to respect a person's efforts. Through my teaching, I have learned the value of feedback, the constructive uses of discipline, and the need for guidelines and limits.

I know that the Washington Cathedral School places great value on both the academic growth of students and their personal development. I share that commitment. I want to participate actively in your school community as a teacher and as an adviser for extracurricular activities such as journalism, wildflower identification, and quilting.

I will provide additional references, an official transcript, or other information upon request. I would like to visit your school and have the opportunity to meet you. I look forward to hearing from you and hope that I can join your school community this fall.

Sincerely,

Rona Shore

Enc: Resume and Course List

Comments: The first sentence attracts attention and draws the reader into the letter, which communicates the enthusiasm and diversity of interests that headmasters look for. Because Rona realizes that this letter will be evaluated as a sample of her writing ability, she makes a special effort to make it interesting.

Employment Inquiry Letter 2

339 Lowell Mail Center
Cambridge, MA 02138-5028
August 24, 1995

Mr. Arnold Q. Bass
President, International Division
Chesebrough-Pond's USA Co.
33 Benedict Place
Greenwich, CT 06830

Dear Mr. Bass:

I am writing to you because I would like to explore opportunities at Chesebrough-Pond's International Division in marketing and public relations for Latin America.

I have majored in Latin American Studies and have lived in Costa Rica. For my senior honors thesis, I did a comparative study of the role of the Catholic church in Mexico and Costa Rica. Awarded a research grant by my department, I spent one month in Mexico City and one month in San Jose interviewing residents and priests in various parishes. I learned a great deal about the role of the church in their lives.

After graduation, I returned to Costa Rica to teach in a Catholic high school in the community where I had done my research. This gave me the opportunity to become completely fluent in Spanish and knowledgeable about the local culture and mores. I became interested in people's reactions to imported consumer goods in the marketplace.

I am intrigued with the challenge of marketing consumer products in a different culture. Although these consumers have some needs and desires similar to ours, their priorities and preferences are different. Consequently, a different marketing approach is appropriate.

I would like the chance to talk with you about international marketing with Chesebrough-Pond's. I will call you next week to arrange a time for us to meet.

Sincerely,

Charles Ramos

Comments: As a result of his career research, Charles has identified an employer and a function to which he brings some special insights. His letter is direct and informative.

Job Application Letter 1

24 Oxford Street
Harvard University
Cambridge, MA 02138
March 11, 1995

Mr. Timothy Borden, Personnel Officer
USGS National Center, MS-215
U.S. Geological Survey
12201 Sunrise Valley Drive
Reston, VA 22092

Dear Mr. Borden:

I am writing to apply for the position of geologist at USGS Headquarters as announced on the Career America College Hotline.

As you can see from the enclosed resume, I am a senior concentrating in earth and planetary sciences at Harvard University. My studies and research in the past four years have focused on geochemistry, particularly as it relates to the late-stage magmatic processes and to the petrology of meteorites. Through my research and work experience during college, I have become proficient in the use of a variety of laboratory equipment, such as the electron microprobe and the scanning electron microscope.

The position of geologist would allow me to utilize my geological knowledge to define and solve problems. I would find this very exciting and challenging.

In addition, I enjoy both creative and technical writing, as well as editing, and take pleasure in designing presentations of technical material.

I will be in the Washington, D.C. area for the week beginning March 25. I would like very much to meet with you at that time to discuss my candidacy for this position.

Sincerely,

Catherine A. Pointer

Comments: In applying for this technical position, Catherine describes her subject interests and her familiarity with laboratory equipment. She also communicates her writing and presentation skills in a way that conveys enthusiasm and confidence.

Job Application Letter 2

4 Chauncy Street
Cambridge, MA 02138
March 4, 1995

Mr. Stephen McCarthy
Creative Services Department
Young and Rubicam, Inc.
285 Madison Avenue
New York, NY 10017

Dear Mr. McCarthy:

I'm the new kid on the advertising block. I may look strange at first, but I think you're going to like me. Here's why:

> I have experience using words and pictures in public communications. In 1990 I wrote the guide to the "Images of Labor" exhibit at the National Museum of American History in Washington, D.C.

> I have an extremely flexible writing style. I have written technical reports for hospital administrators and union officials, and recently presented a thesis to the most intellectually demanding history department in the nation.

> I know how to sell ideas. As a teaching fellow at Harvard, I developed audiovisual presentations and dramatized historical events in order to promote enthusiasm about the past. And when all else failed, my sense of humor proved to be an ace in the hole.

I have enclosed two writing samples for your perusal. The first consists of the sketches I wrote for the National Museum's art exhibit. These have since been published in Moe Foner, ed., *Images of Labor* (New York: Pilgrim Press, 1991). The second is a chapter of my thesis, a dramatic reconstruction of a riot which occurred more than one hundred years ago.

I am a person who writes simply and succinctly, who enjoys working with people, and who prefers to make history rather than simply write about it. This is why I am interested in becoming an advertising copywriter.

I would like to meet with you to talk about the copywriting position at Young and Rubicam as advertised in *Adweek*. I will call next week to find out when that might be possible.

Sincerely,

Adam Devereaux

Comments: This letter is appropriate for the advertising field. Adam sells his writing ability through this letter and the writing samples which he attaches. The uniqueness of the letter illustrates his creativity.

Job Application Letter 3

Elaine duBarry
McKinsey & Company, Inc.
55 East 52nd Street
New York, NY 10022

November 11, 1994

Dear Ms. duBarry:

I would like to apply for an Associate position with McKinsey & Company. I have a Ph.D. in Neuroscience from Stanford University, and am currently a Postdoctoral Research Associate in Neurobiology at Brown University. I learned about your work in health care by attending the discussion at The Charles Hotel in Cambridge on November 4.

Your Associates' presentation really caught my interest. How rewarding it would be to have impact while addressing a variety of tough, complex problems. I welcome the opportunity to achieve measurable goals while working closely with a team of top management and creative, motivated peers.

My primary qualifications for Associate derive from my experience as a research scientist interested in the brain:
- a liking for complex problems
- an ability to locate and distill a broad range of information and to generate fact-based hypotheses in the face of ambiguity and complexity
- an ability to test a hypothesis and to interpret results objectively
- an ability to communicate clearly and persuasively

My familiarity with the world of biomedical research may also prove useful.

My office preferences are as follows: First choices are Boston and Stamford; second choices are Bedminster, Pittsburgh, San Francisco, San Jose, Minneapolis, and Montreal. I would consider other options as well.

Thank you for your consideration. I look forward to hearing from you.

Sincerely,

Lorraine G. Perry, Ph.D.
Dept. of Neuroscience, Box C-L
Brown University
Providence, RI 02912

401-863-9244
FAX: 401-863-0910
lperry@brownvm.brown.edu

Comments: After stating how she learned about McKinsey's work in health care, Lorraine expresses enthusiasm for the company. In the third paragraph she translates and highlights the skills she developed as a research scientist which are important in consulting.

Job Application Letter 4

42 Leverett Mail Center
Cambridge, MA 02138-6034
April 19, 1995

Maureen S. Bosley
J.P. Morgan & Co., Inc.
23 Wall Street
New York, NY 10260-0023

Dear Ms. Bosley:

I am writing to express my interest in the consulting position in Management Services at J.P. Morgan. I expect to receive my degree in history and literature with honors in June 1995.

Recently I completed my senior thesis, a yearlong research and writing project. This undertaking allowed me to improve my planning and problem-solving skills. My work this past summer at the law offices of O'Neill and Sullivan provided me with an opportunity to write reports sent directly to clients in a deadline-oriented environment, an experience I found invaluable.

As captain of the women's varsity swim team, I have exercised diligence, leadership skills, and a commitment to specific goals. Since I was not recruited for the team, my ability was far below that of my teammates when I joined as a freshman. But through hard work and determination, I am now one of the fastest swimmers, and was honored last year with the "Most Improved" award and election as captain.

I am excited to learn about the financial markets, and I believe my organizational and leadership skills will be well suited to a career in management at J.P. Morgan.

Sincerely,

Patricia Doucette

Comments: The third paragraph of this letter is unique and personal and tells the reader a lot about Patricia. The weakness in the letter is her failure to express enthusiasm for J.P. Morgan, which prides itself on being a great place to work.

Job Application Letter 5

352 Quincy Mail Center
Cambridge, MA 02138-6609
November 30, 1994

June Salerno
Research Manager
CTW Magazine Research
One Lincoln Plaza
New York, NY 10023

Dear Ms. Salerno:

Thank you for sending me information about your magazine research internships (my Office of Career Services also sends thanks for the new copy of your data sheet). As I mentioned on the telephone, I am a junior at Harvard University majoring in English and interested in pursuing a career in education through media. I have always admired the work of the Children's Television Workshop and am extremely interested in your summer internship.

I believe that my current and past jobs have given me skills useful for the research your department conducts. I have worked extensively with children both as a baby-sitter and nanny and as a counselor at a nursery day-camp. As a professor's research assistant, I have gained experience in compiling and synthesizing information. As an office assistant, I am responsible for dealing with co-workers and clients on the telephone, entering data into a computer, and writing and editing letters and memos. Perhaps most importantly, as I think my academic record indicates, I am an extremely well-organized and dedicated student. I promise I would bring the same energy and enthusiasm which I devote to my studies to the work I would do for you.

I will be visiting my parents in New York from December 21 until January 3, and would love to meet with you at that time. I will call you next week to see if this is convenient for you. Thank you in advance.

Sincerely,

Margot Vanderhorn

Comments: Applying for a summer internship, this letter is a follow-up to a telephone inquiry. The letter highlights Margot's work experiences that are relevant to magazine research. The first paragraph would be improved if the sentence about OCS in parentheses were omitted.

Comments (opposite page): This is a very targeted comprehensive description of the experience and qualifications that Suzanne brings to the analyst position. Some employers might find it too long, but it is concise and packed with information.

Job Application Letter 6

289 Kirkland Mail Center
Cambridge, MA 02138-5912
April 14, 1995

Ms. Martha Petit, Associate
J.P. Morgan & Co. Incorporated
23 Wall Street
New York, NY 10260-0023

Dear Ms. Petit:

I am a senior at Harvard concentrating in East Asian Studies and would like to apply for the Management Services analyst position. I have always enjoyed researching, analyzing, and solving problems and would like the opportunity to explore these interests in consulting because I find the field exciting and challenging.

At Harvard, I have acquired many of the skills that would allow me to be an effective analyst. Whereas many majors focus on only one field, East Asian Studies has allowed me to study a wide range of fields which have included economics, government, history, sociology, and language studies. In my senior honors thesis, I analyzed labor-management relations at Japanese auto factories located in the U.S. Through these academic experiences, I have developed strong oral and written communication skills, extensive research capabilities, and crucial problem-solving skills which enable me to identify and analyze a problem carefully.

Through my extracurricular activities and work experiences, I have also acquired some invaluable skills. In particular, my academic and work experiences in Japan were enriching. During the fall semester of my junior year, I studied abroad in Kobe, Japan, participated in a home-stay program, and had the opportunity to travel throughout the country. This past summer, I worked for a Diet member in his Okayama office and participated in a national election campaign. Furthermore, I organized and conducted educational seminars and interviewed government bureaucrats for senior thesis research. Through creativity, patience, and perseverance, I learned how to adapt, communicate, and work cooperatively in an unfamiliar international environment, while always maintaining a good sense of humor.

As co-chair of the Chinatown Committee, a public service organization which services the Boston Chinatown community, and as director of the Chinatown Big Sibling Program, I was personally responsible for the successful operation of several programs. These responsibilities and my work experiences in various office environments have required that I be creative and resourceful and that I maintain strong organizational and communication skills. Whether I am studying, participating in extracurricular activities, or working, I am dedicated, self-motivated, and set a high standard for myself. I work well under pressure in both independent and team efforts.

I am very interested in working as an analyst for J.P. Morgan Management Services. I have enclosed a copy of my resume and would appreciate it if you would consider my candidacy. I look forward to meeting with you and discussing the position in greater detail.

Sincerely,

Suzanne Chan

Thank-You Letter 1

217 Jasmine Street
Boston, MA 02115
October 25, 1994

William Sorenson
ABC Company
333 Smith Street
Boston, MA 02127

Dear Mr. Sorenson:

Thank you for meeting with me yesterday to discuss careers in real estate. I greatly appreciate your sharing some of your experiences in this field with me.

I was interested to learn that you think that getting some initial experience in selling and renting space lays a strong foundation for a career in commercial real estate. I think that I would enjoy being a salesman.

I enjoyed our conversation and hope that we might be able to meet again sometime. I will keep you informed of my progress as I explore this exciting career.

Sincerely yours,

Alan Cortes

Comments: Thank-you letters should be short and should be sent promptly. It is best to speak specifically about some aspect of the interview and what it meant to you.

Thank-You Letter 2

456 Cabot Mail Center
Cambridge, MA 02138-1560
March 10, 1995

Mr. Jason Crawford
Goldman Sachs and Co.
85 Broad Street
New York, NY 10004-2434

Dear Mr. Crawford:

Thank you for giving me the opportunity to talk with you about my interest in Goldman Sachs yesterday. I enjoyed meeting with you, as I have with all the people from your firm.

The intense competitiveness and hard-driving environment of the investment banking business makes it very attractive to me. I thrive on teamwork and competition. As I mentioned yesterday, I have been swimming competitively for twelve years. As captain of the Harvard team this year, I had the thrill of leading our team to the NCAA Finals.

If you need additional information, please do not hesitate to call me at (617) 493-1234.

Sincerely yours,

Marilyn Donaldson

Comments: Thank-you letters following job interviews should express interest in the job. Marilyn also uses this letter to restate her enthusiasm for teamwork and competition as documented by her success as a competitive swimmer.

Thank-You Letter 3

27A Pythagoras Street
Cambridge, MA 02138
March 12, 1995

Dr. Heather Maguire
Headmaster
The Bridgeton School
Sterling, MA 01564

Dear Dr. Maguire:

I enjoyed meeting you and members of your faculty on Thursday. I am
most enthusiastic about the history teacher position at The Bridgeton School.

I was particularly impressed with your concern for the individuality of
every student and your innovative programs for responding to their varied
needs. The students in the class that I observed seemed to be engaged,
enthusiastic, and well prepared. It was a delight to see the way that Mr. Smith
reached out to involve every student.

I would love to have the opportunity to be a member of your faculty.
Thank you for considering my candidacy. If there is any further information I
can provide, please let me know. I look forward to hearing from you.

Sincerely yours,

Jane Murray

Comments: By describing what impressed her during her job interview and school
visit, Jane is communicating what she values in a teacher and a school.

Job Acceptance Letter

099 Mather Mail Center
Cambridge, MA 02138-6175
May 12, 1995

Mr. Joseph Lawrence
Manager of College Relations
Morgan Stanley & Co. Inc.
1251 Avenue of the Americas
New York, NY 10020-1104

Dear Mr. Lawrence:

I am very pleased to accept your offer of a position as a Financial Analyst at the annual salary of $38,000. I have been very impressed with everyone whom I have met during my interviews and I look forward to joining your staff.

As we discussed, I will report for work on August 1. Before that date, I will have a physical examination and submit the report to you. During the next month, I will complete my move to New York City and I hope to have some time to join my family for a vacation on the Cape. If you need to contact me before August 1, my parents will know how to reach me. Their telephone number is (508) 222-6666.

Thank you for everything that you did to make the interviewing process such a pleasant experience. I am very excited to have the opportunity to become a part of Morgan Stanley.

Sincerely yours,

Janice Mitchell

Comments: In a job acceptance letter it is important to express enthusiasm and to describe how and when you will meet your obligations prior to starting work.

Letter Declining an Offer

352 Charles Street
Boston, MA 02114
April 27, 1995

Mr. John Fulton
Manager of College Relations
The Boston Consulting Group, Inc.
Exchange Place
Boston, MA 02109

Dear Mr. Fulton:

I was pleased that I was able to reach you by telephone to tell you that I was declining your job offer. I am grateful that you understand my decision and honored by the thought that I will always be welcome at BCG.

Everyone that I met at your firm was wonderful, which made this decision very tough. As I stated on the phone, I have accepted a position with Corporate Strategies where I will be an Associate with the oil and gas industry practice.

I want to thank you again for all your help and support during my job search.

Best regards,

Aaron Scheingold

Comments: A letter declining a job offer will usually follow a telephone call. It should be friendly, positive, and short.

Comments (opposite page): There are many reasons you might decide to write a follow-up letter. In this case, James wants to assert strongly his interest in a position that might frequently be filled by someone more junior than he. He wants to convince the committee that he will not feel underemployed.

Follow-Up Letter 1

650 W. 122nd St., Apt. 4G
New York, NY 10027
26 January 1995

Dean of Students Search
Office of Human Resources
University of Pennsylvania
Philadelphia, PA 19104

Dear Members of the Search Committee:

Last Friday at our weekly departmental staff meeting I told Don Gibson here at Columbia University (and one of my references), that I had just learned of and applied for the Dean of Students position at the University of Pennsylvania. He was very ready and happy to support me (indeed, I think he will be writing you about my candidacy soon), but he did say one thing that worried me: "You know they're very possibly going to think that you're too senior for the position." He knows as well as I do that at Penn, as at Columbia and Yale, this sort of position has increasingly, almost by default, become the province of junior scholars who, for whatever reasons, leave the tenure track early or never get on it in the first place.

I didn't speak to this *de facto* situation in my letter of application to you (dated January 17), but Professor Gibson's comment leads me to think I should have. May I address it now?

Let me begin by stating quite simply that this is most certainly the kind of work I want to do. I'm deeply committed to undergraduate education. I've never been happier in my career than when teaching and advising undergraduates at Columbia, where students and faculty share a genuine commitment to and enthusiasm for learning. I've had a chance to discover—and to demonstrate, at great professional risk—that I value the fostering of education and learning far above the trappings of academic rank and prestige and the comforts of tenured security. What's more, I enjoy administrative work, and I have a consistent record of administrative effectiveness both inside and outside academe. Increasingly at Columbia I have learned how very fulfilling to me a meaningful position in academic administration can be; I'm eager now to put my commitment into practice.

Yes, I have a good bit of academic experience, and a senior scholar's academic credentials. But let me put the issue of my atypical candidacy succinctly: would you prefer that your candidates *not* have such experience and credentials?

I truly believe that I would enjoy the Dean of Students position and perform its duties well. I even believe that my academic background would give me some strong advantages in filling the Dean of Students role. Again, thank you for considering me for it. I look forward to hearing from you.

Sincerely,

James Hudson

Follow-Up Letter 2

September 18, 1994

Dear Marty,

I just wanted to let you know that I left the Sheffield Arts Collaborative in August and am now attending Georgetown University Law Center. I am very happy about my decision and excited to be part of Georgetown. Thanks for all your help and advice.

Best,

Diane Sarton '87

Comments (above): A short, newsy update handwritten on notepaper can mean a lot to your past advisers. Diane omitted her home address from the letter but it was on the envelope in case the receiver wanted to respond.

Comments (opposite page): Employers are impressed by a candidate who singles out their company and persists in seeking an interview. This letter did get James an interview with Blackwood Hill in New York City.

Follow-Up Letter 3

264 Dunster Mail Center
Cambridge, MA 02138-6169
February 27, 1995

George Logan
Blackwood Hill and Associates
88 Broad Street - Suite 3300
New York, NY 10004

Dear Mr. Logan:

I was very disappointed that I was not granted an interview for the financial analyst position through the on-campus recruiting process at Harvard, and I am writing to reiterate both my interest in Blackwood Hill and my qualifications for the job.

During your information meeting in November, you listed, among other things, "intelligence, maturity, self-confidence, leadership qualities, drive, and goal-orientation" as specific qualities that your firm seeks in analyst candidates. Furthermore, you have mentioned that good grades are obviously preferable to average grades, but that the trend of the G.P.A. is also significant.

I believe I have both the tangible and intangible skills to meet the demands of the financial analyst position. As my resume indicates, my grades have been quite respectable, and they have consistently improved—even while working 15 hours a week termtime to defray the cost of my education. In addition to an honors curriculum in Government, I have enjoyed several electives in economics and statistics.

Moreover, I believe my success in squash and my position as co-captain of Harvard's varsity squash team demonstrate my work ethic, leadership capacity, and ability to overcome adversity. This letter, I think, shows my perseverance.

I became interested in investment banking after studying the market for corporate control in a course on industrial organization, and after spending last summer as a research analyst for Kidder Peabody.

Why am I interested in Blackwood Hill? Although I attended several investment banking information sessions last fall, Blackwood Hill was the only firm which consistently emphasized the significance of its principles and its culture. These features have been maintained, I supposed, due to Blackwood's autonomy in an era when others have been eager to combine. I really sensed an environment of excellence at Blackwood, and would be eager to contribute to it. Friends who have worked on Wall Street have only reinforced these impressions.

I sincerely hope you reconsider my application and give me the opportunity to speak to you or any other recruiter. Thank you very much for your time and consideration. I shall call you in a few days to see how we should proceed.

Sincerely,

James Whittle

REQUESTING LETTERS OF RECOMMENDATION

Whom to Ask

The best people to write letters of recommendation for you are professors, instructors, employers, and advisers who have supervised and evaluated work of which you are proud. It is important that the person know you well. If you keep in touch with your favorite teachers and employers over the years and share with them the development of your plans, they will appreciate having the opportunity to write letters that may assist you in progressing toward your goals.

If the letter of recommendation that you are requesting is for a specific purpose, you should identify potential letter writers who have had the opportunity to observe you developing and utilizing skills and talents which will be valued in that selection process. You will almost always want an academic reference written by a professor or a tutor who can describe your approach to learning, analytic and problem-solving abilities, and written and oral communication skills. You may also want a letter from someone who can comment on other personal strengths, leadership and interpersonal skills, and work characteristics such as initiative, enthusiasm, attention to detail, and high standards of performance. It is most helpful if they are familiar with and can describe specific examples. All letter writers should address your potential for success in the given field.

As you complete a course, an extracurricular activity, or a job in which you are proud of your achievement, you may want to request a general letter of recommendation from your professor, supervisor, or employer. If you find it difficult or awkward to request letters, remember that anyone who teaches or supervises the work of others expects to be asked to serve as a reference. The advantage of requesting a letter at the time you complete the course or the job is that your performance is fresh in the mind of the letter writer, and therefore he can speak specifically about your accomplishments. There is also the advantage that you are in contact with him, whereas later on you might have difficulty finding him.

Sometime in the future, you may want to ask those who wrote general letters of recommendation for you to rewrite their letters for a specific purpose. This is not a burdensome task for the writer. The major effort is the development of the first letter of recommendation about you; future editions require very little time.

How to Ask

Because you want letters that are positive and supportive, you should always give the person the opportunity to tell you if he does not think he is the best person to write for you, or that he does not know you well enough, or that he is too busy.

The best way to ask for a letter of recommendation is in a personal conference so that you have the opportunity to gauge the likelihood that the person will write a strong letter. If you ask, "Do you feel that you know me well enough to write a strong letter?" and watch the person's body language as well as what they say, you will get an indication of how enthusiastic he is about supporting your candidacy. If you sense hesitancy, you may want to suggest that perhaps it would be best if you ask someone else.

If it is not possible to meet with the person, the choice between making your request by telephone or by letter depends upon your relationship with the person. It is a choice based on what you feel is the best substitute for a personal conference.

When you request a letter, be sure that you share your goals and aspirations and the reasons why you are making the application that you are asking him to support. Discuss with him how this opportunity will help you progress towards your long-range goals.

What Information to Provide

It is important that you think through carefully what information will be helpful to the person who is writing a letter for you. You should refresh the letter writer's memory of the work that you have done for him. If some time has passed since you completed this work, you may want to supply materials such as the research paper you wrote or the special project that you completed. You may also want to give a progress report on relevant experiences since that time.

For a letter of reference for a specific application, you should supply the letter writer with information about the criteria used in the selection process. This will make it possible for him to describe the qualities in which the employer is most interested.

The other kind of information you want to supply is information about yourself. A copy of your resume, your transcript, and a draft of your application essay will assist the writer in viewing you and speaking of you in a broader context.

The Deadline

Be sure to inform your letter writer of the deadline for the receipt of letters of recommendation. Request your letter two to four weeks ahead of the deadline, if possible. It is important to provide a stamped, addressed envelope for the letter and a written note stating to whom the letter should be addressed and the deadline.

Remember that your letter writers have many other responsibilities to fulfill and other deadlines to meet. It is perfectly acceptable to follow up a few days before the deadline to be sure that your letter of recommendation has been sent or that it has been received. Making certain that your application is complete by the deadline is your responsibility.

Confidentiality

Since the enactment of the Family Educational Rights and Privacy Act of 1974, a person has the legal right to read letters of recommendation written about him unless he waives that right.

Some recipients consider a confidential letter to be a more honest and accurate appraisal of a candidate; in fact, you may find that confidential letters are strongly preferred in some cases. However, you may want to be able to read your letters in order to select which letters to use for a particular purpose, depending on which of your qualities are discussed.

The issue of whether or not to waive your right to read your letters is complicated. It is your decision to make. You may find it helpful to discuss your options with a career counselor or academic adviser.

INTERVIEWING FOR JOBS

An interview is a conversation with a purpose. The interview provides you the opportunity to convince the employer that you are the best candidate for the position he must fill. You, the interviewee, share the responsibility for making the interview productive. You can be helpful to the employer by answering the following questions:

Can you do the job? Do you have the skills or can you learn the skills to do this job? What in your past experience is relevant to predicting that you can learn to do this job?

Do you want to do this job? Are you highly motivated to do this job well? How does this job fit into your long-range goals? Will you invest your best effort toward outstanding performance in this job?

Will you fit in? Will you work well with other team members whose work is related to yours? Will you be productive?

If you have researched the job and the organization as discussed in Chapter 4, you should be able to discuss these questions effectively. Select past achievements that most clearly document that you can fulfill the responsibilities of this position and that you will fit in well in this organization. Practice recounting these experience(s) in a short and concise form.

Most employers want employees who are energetic, enthusiastic, responsible, and thoughtful of others. They want employees who approach new situations with confidence, learn quickly, and are willing to take initiative. They also want employees who communicate clearly, listen carefully, express themselves concisely, and are reliable and honest. All of these qualities can be demonstrated in the interview.

The information exchanged in an interview is not all verbalized. Your appearance, manner, and voice—your total presence—communicate aspects of your qualifications and suitability for the job. Your behavior in the interview is taken as a brief sample of how you will conduct yourself on the job.

Types of Interviews

The first interview for a job is often a screening interview and may be conducted on campus. The second interview or interviews are usually conducted on site by the supervisors and perhaps by potential colleagues. Sometimes you will be interviewed over lunch, and sometimes in a group. It is helpful to be aware of the objectives of each of these types of interviews.

The purpose of the **screening interview** is to screen out applicants who are not qualified and to select the applicants who would seem to be the best prospects for making a contribution to the organization. Emphasis is placed on whether you will be compatible with people in the organization. This is a subjective judgment made by the interviewer based on how much he enjoyed meeting and conversing with you. The interviewer also makes a judgment about how interested you are in his organization. To demonstrate your interest, you need to have researched the organization and to be able to converse knowledgeably about it.

The **second interview** or interviews are usually held in the place of employment and constitute your opportunity to meet the supervisor and colleagues with whom you will be working. Any information that you can learn ahead of time about these people will be helpful to you. In these interviews, the interviewers are trying to decide if you are the best qualified person of all those whom they are interviewing. Each person that you meet and talk with will be asked to evaluate your suitability for this job.

The **lunch interview** is usually programmed to be a more personal and informal interview than the others, and is often held with potential colleagues rather than with supervisors. Remember that those who take you to lunch will also be asked to evaluate your candidacy. It is not advisable to engage in conversation about intimate personal matters or controversial subjects. If you are asked personal questions which you prefer not to answer, it is best to pass over them lightly and respond with a question on a different subject. Probably the best topic of conversation is one of mutual interest. It is perfectly acceptable to use this opportunity to ask what these people enjoy most about working for this organization and to try to gain some insight into what work would be like for you on this job. It is usually best not to have a drink at lunch and not to order a meal that might be messy to eat.

Sometimes you will be given a **group interview** with other candidates present. This is a difficult kind of interview because your behavior is being evaluated in relation to the other candidates as well as toward the interviewer. You will have to judge how aggressive or outspoken you should be. In this situation it is probably best to demonstrate that you are a good team member, that you listen to others, and that you think about and respond to their contributions. Even when the stated purpose of the group meeting is to give you information about the organization, your behavior is being observed.

Another type of interview is the **committee interview**, where you are the only candidate present and you are being interviewed by several people. This is a very challenging kind of interview because you will be trying to respond accurately and appropriately to four or five individuals. The best approach is usually to make eye contact with the person asking the question while he is asking it, so that you can be thinking through your response. While you are making your response, your attention will be primarily on the questioner, but you should look around to see whether you have the attention and support of other members of the interviewing group. When you go into a group interview, it is particularly important that you try to have some knowledge of the names, positions, and backgrounds of each of the interviewers.

Styles of Interviews

In general, there are four different interviewing styles: directive, nondirective, stress, and unplanned.

In the **directive interview**, the interviewer will ask you questions. He may be asking exactly the same questions of every candidate. You should answer each question with the most relevant information you can select and keep your answers short and concise. Before the interview ends, the interviewer will probably ask you if you have any questions, and you should make sure that you have some questions to ask at that time.

One type of question often used in interviews for jobs in consulting is the "case question." To learn how well you think on your feet, the interviewer will outline a problem and ask how you would solve it. His objective is to learn how your mind works and how well you function under pressure. He is interested less in your answer, and more in how you approach solving the problem. It is important to remember that the interviewers may ask case questions for which they have no answer.

The **nondirective interview** will start with an open-ended question, such as, "Tell me about yourself." This is not an invitation to relate your life history, but it gives you the opportunity to tell the interviewer why you are qualified for the job. Even though the opening is a very comprehensive one, you should not give a long response, but attempt to initiate a conversation. Keep any answer limited to about two to three minutes in length. Start with a few observations about what you think the job requires and why you think you can do it, and then ask the interviewer what he thinks is most important about the job. Usually the nondirective interviewer is seeking a more informal exchange and will be glad to respond to your questions throughout the interview.

In **stress interviews**, the interviewer will ask you questions which are very difficult to answer or which have no answer. He is intentionally putting you under pressure to test whether you are able to control your emotions and retain your composure. The answer that you give is not as important as your behavior. It is very important that you maintain your composure. Another type of question which puts you under stress is the one posed by the interviewer who asks you to take a position on a certain issue and then disagrees with the stance you have taken. In this case, it is best to defend your position, but moderately, so that you show strength of conviction but not an unwillingness to consider other points of view. Stress interviews are not used very commonly, but may be appropriate when the job is one which requires you to perform under stress.

The fourth kind of interview is the **unplanned interview** by the inexperienced interviewer. This interviewer will seem to be uncomfortable with his role. Your objective should be to help make him comfortable and to give him the information which he will need to make hiring decisions. You will need to take the initiative in this kind of interview, but that does not mean you should conduct a monologue. Try to develop a conversation which gives you the opportunity to communicate your qualifications, but which also gives the interviewer the opportunity to participate.

Preparing for Interviews

Get as much information ahead of time as you can about the job, organization, and interviewer. Organizations are unique; you want to understand the personality of this particular one so that you can tailor your presentation. The interview only gives time for the employer to get a glimpse of you. Be sure that the glimpse includes the kind of information about you that he needs in order to feel confident that you are the best candidate for the job.

How you prepare for an interview depends on your work style. For some people, writing out answers to questions that they expect to be asked is helpful, but if this would lead you to memorize answers and deliver them by rote, it will be counterproductive. Some people outline or list the points they want to make about why they want the job and the relevant accomplishments that illustrate their qualifications. Some people find it helpful to practice with a friend or an adviser, responding to questions such as those listed later in this chapter.

Video interview training is very helpful because it gives you the opportunity to observe your interview posture and behavior as well as hear your responses to questions. Some college career service offices offer video interview training sessions.

You should plan to take extra copies of your resume to the interview. Also be sure that you have a notebook and pen in case you want to make some notes. You may want to take samples of your work if you think that they are relevant to the requirements of the job. If possible, be prepared to leave these copies of your published articles, software programs, or videos with the interviewer.

Plan to arrive early, so that you have time to relax and collect your thoughts before the scheduled time of the interview.

General Outline of an Interview

The impression that you make as you enter the interviewing room is lasting. Your attire should be appropriate for the job for which you are applying. Your stance and stride should express confidence. Your handshake, eye contact, and self-introduction, "Mr. Jones, I'm Jane Smith. It's a pleasure to meet you," should express energy, enthusiasm, and anticipation.

Usually the interviewer will open the interview with informal conversation about a mutual interest, the weather, or some topic which he hopes will help you feel at ease. This opening conversation will give you some indication of the style of interview that you are going to have. This part of the interview is very much like the kind of conversation that takes place between any two people who have just been introduced to each other.

In the main body of the interview, the interviewer is responsible for the format or style. Usually he will initiate the substantive part of the interview with a question, but if you find the opening stretching out, it is acceptable to initiate conversation about your qualifications for the job. You should adapt your behavior to the interviewer's style and pace. Listen carefully to his questions and respond with the most pertinent, relevant information you can, taking a moment to organize your thoughts, if necessary.

The content of the interview is mostly up to you. Remember that the employer wants to get to know you. He wants to understand your work values and career aspirations. It is not your past experiences per se that are important, but how you approached each opportunity, what you accomplished, and how you reflect on what you learned from the experience. If you convince him that you put forth your best effort in academic or nonacademic responsibilities in the past, he will assume that you are ready to make that kind of commitment to your work in his organization.

Many employers ask what you would like to be doing in five or ten years. Don't be misled by this question! They do not expect you to name a job title and income level in their organization. They do want to know whether you have given some thought to your future and what kinds of aspirations you have. It is appropriate to be quite general in your response, but to communicate that you look forward to advancing in your field.

Your objective is to make the interview a shared conversation, so it is perfectly all right to complete your response with a question for the interviewer. For example, if the interviewer started the interview with the question, "Tell me about yourself," you might respond with a brief statement of how you became interested in the job and why you think you will enjoy it, and conclude with a question to the interviewer about the job.

Usually the interviewer will take responsibility for closing the interview. He will probably give you some evaluation of the interview, and he should most certainly outline what the next step will be. If the interviewer does not offer you information about how the job search is being conducted and when you can expect to hear about another interview or about the final selection, it is appropriate for you to ask for this information before concluding the interview. Ideally, the interview will have been a conversation that both have enjoyed, and you will conclude by telling each other so.

It is important that you write a **thank-you note after each interview**. (See the Writing Letters section.) This gives you the opportunity to express, once again, your interest in the job, and perhaps to comment briefly on a topic in the interview that you felt was covered incompletely or a question that was raised but was not answered by you at that time. Your thank-you note should be brief.

Questions Frequently Asked by Employers

The following is just a sampling of questions that you might be asked. If you think about how you will answer these questions to give the employer the information he needs about you, you will be prepared for most interviews.

- What is the accomplishment of which you are most proud?
- What do you see yourself doing five years from now? Ten years from now?
- Why do you think you are qualified for this position?
- Tell me about yourself.
- What are your special strengths and weaknesses?
- How would your friends describe you?

- Why did you study for a Ph.D. in history?
- Why did you concentrate in Romance languages?
- What did you learn from (some experience on resume)?
- Why did you compete to write for your campus newspaper?
- How did playing varsity football help prepare you for your future career?
- Do you plan to go to graduate school?

- What were the best and worst aspects of (a previous job)?
- In what kind of work environment do you work the best?
- What kind of people do you like to work with?
- Why have you chosen a career in _____?
- What would be your ideal job?
- Why are you changing careers?
- How do you think your degree in liberal arts can help you in this job?
- Why are you interested in our firm?
- Who are our firm's biggest competitors? What can we do to improve our market share?

You might also be asked a role-play question such as how you would handle a hypothetical situation that you might encounter in the position for which you are a candidate.

Questions You Might Want to Ask the Interviewer

You already have experience in asking employers questions about careers from your career exploration interviews. The difference in questions you might ask in a job interview is that they should be pertinent to the job you are applying for or demonstrate that you are interested in the organization as a whole.

Here are a few examples:

- What are the career opportunities in this organization for people who start in this position?
- How are job assignments decided at the end of the training program?
- How are projects allocated among the staff?
- I read in *Newsweek* that your company is having difficulty in European markets. Was this article accurate? How is your company responding?
- I understand that you have just introduced a new product/service. How has it been received so far?
- I'm interested in learning more about the company's new technology that was mentioned in the *Wall Street Journal* last week.
- Your organization has many prominent individuals on its board of trustees. What impact do they have on the organization?

It is best not to ask about salary, vacation, and benefits until you are offered the job. There will be time for detailed questions and negotiation later in the process if you receive an offer.

Responding to Illegal or Inappropriate Questions

Federal regulations prohibit employment interviewers from asking questions about age, race, religion, ethnic origin, or arrest record (asking about convictions is legal, but not about arrests). In most states there are regulations against asking about marital status, family, day care arrangements, or a spouse's career unless the information relates to performance of the job. However, sometimes these questions are asked.

Before you start interviewing, you should decide how you plan to respond to questions about your personal life. You can state that you think the question is not job related and refuse to answer it. You can respond, "I'm not sure I understand the relevance of your question to the job. If your concern is about my ability to fulfill the requirements of this job, I can assure you that I feel confident that I can." You can make a noncommittal reply and ask a question that returns the conversation to a job-related topic. You can answer the question, giving information about your personal life. If you are interested in a job, the second and third options are most likely to result in a positive interview.

Some examples of nonanswers are:

Are you interested in marriage and children? Right now I am interested in getting started in my career. I have always thought I would marry, but if I do, it will be later. (Return to some previous topic, for instance: What are the opportunities for advancement with your firm?)

Do you have a girlfriend/boyfriend? I have close friends whose company I enjoy. If you hire me for this job and I move to New York, I am sure I will develop new friendships there.

Who will take care of your children while you are at work? I have made arrangements for the care of my children and am prepared to fulfill the responsibilities of my job. Who would my supervisor be in this position?

You should be able to think of responses which make clear to the interviewer without embarrassing him that you are not prepared to answer illegal questions or engage in a discussion of personal matters with him. If the interviewer returns repeatedly to inappropriate topics, you may want to end the interview.

After the interview, you will want to assess whether the illegal or inappropriate questions are indications of a work environment or company policies to which you object. If you feel the employer does not observe fair employment practices, you probably will not want to work for him. If the interviewer persisted in asking illegal questions, you may also want to explore whether you have grounds for filing a legal complaint.

Good Luck!

Every interview is a unique adventure. Be prepared to be engaging and spontaneous.

- **Be yourself at your professional best.** Present those aspects of yourself which best meet the employer's needs.
- **Act confident (but not cocky).** That will help you feel confident.
- **Listen carefully.** Be sure you understand a question before you answer it.
- **Ask perceptive questions.** When reading company literature, prepare questions that will show you have thought analytically about the company's current status or future direction.
- **Let your enthusiasm show.** Be energetic and responsive. These are qualities that employers value.

INTERVIEWING FOR INFORMATION

Meeting with someone to learn about his career experiences is commonly referred to as an "information interview." It seems more appropriate to think of it as a "career conversation," because the objective is not solely to get information and advice from this person about his career. The objective is to get to know each other and, if you become interested in each other, to lay the foundation for an ongoing relationship.

Because you initiated the contact, you are responsible for the structure and progress of the interview. The roles are the reverse of those in the job interview. You are the interviewer and the focus of the interview is on the career adviser. You need to have prepared what you want to learn from the adviser as well as what you want him to learn about you.

As discussed in Chapter 2, you need to research the person, company, and industry before you meet with a career adviser. It is a waste of a valuable opportunity to spend time in an interview asking about information that you could easily have read. Your goal in this conversation is to learn about this person's career experiences and perspectives on the future—you want to gain "insider information" that you could never find in print. To be prepared for this kind of conversation, you need to have done your homework.

As in the job interview, you should greet the adviser with a firm handshake, make eye contact, and call him by name. You should be dressed appropriately for the workplace. (The previous section, Interviewing for Jobs, gives general advice on interviewing that you will find helpful.) An efficient way to give the adviser an overview of your experiences and interests is to hand him a copy of your resume. While he is scanning your resume, you can start the conversation by giving a brief description of your interest in his career field.

Your initial question should be about what the adviser finds rewarding and satisfying in his work. If you begin by asking him to be reflective about his daily work and career, the conversation will be more interesting to you both. As the conversation proceeds, don't hesitate to participate by mentioning reflections of your own, but keep your remarks very brief so that most of the time you are listening, not talking.

Respect the person's time. If the appointment was for a half hour, begin to close the interview after about twenty-five minutes by expressing your appreciation for all you have learned and by asking if there are any people that he would recommend that you contact. Ask what you should be reading to learn about the field. If you would like to have the opportunity to spend some time with him to observe or participate in his working day, this is the time to ask.

After the interview, write a **thank-you note**. Make notes of what you have learned and record your impressions of the person and workplace.

Scheduling a First Meeting by Telephone

To request the opportunity to meet with a potential career adviser, you may telephone directly or write a letter to him and follow up with a telephone call. You should plan these telephone calls carefully. The following scripts may help you get started.

1. Introduce yourself and tell him where you got his name:

    "Hello, this is Mary Smith. Joe Murray suggested that I call you." Or, "I found your name in the alumni career adviser files at the Office of Career Services." Or, "I met you briefly at the reception last Friday."

2. Explain why you are calling.

202 / Career Development Skills

"I am calling to ask if you would meet with me to help me learn about careers in consulting." Or, "I am graduating next June and I am trying to decide whether to focus my job search on consulting or banking. I have arranged my schedule so that I have no classes on Thursdays. Would it be possible to schedule a meeting on a Thursday in the next few weeks?"

3a. If the answer is yes, repeat the time and the place of the interview. Express your appreciation.

"Next Thursday, the 12th of October will be fine. Shall I come directly to your office? Thank you, I will look forward to meeting you."

3b. If he responds that this is a busy time and asks what you would like to know, restate the kind of information and advice that you are seeking and state that even 15 minutes would be helpful.

"What I hope to learn is what you have found rewarding and satisfying in your work as a consultant. I would also appreciate your advice on my job-hunting strategy. Just 15 minutes of your time would be helpful to me."

4. If the response is positive, confirm the date and express your appreciation as in 3a. If the response is still negative, ask if he has a few minutes to talk with you now.

"I am sorry that it is not possible for us to meet in the near future. Do you have a few minutes now to answer a question or two?" (If yes) "I would be interested in what you find most rewarding in your work as a consultant." Other questions will follow logically, but include a question about what professional literature he reads and other people that he would suggest that you talk to about consulting.

5a. Be sensitive to the fact that you have interrupted him during a work day. Ask only a few questions and then close by thanking him for his time.

"Your advice has been most helpful and I greatly appreciate you taking the time to talk with me. I will continue to research the consulting industry as you suggest and will call the people you mentioned. May I call you again after I have made progress in my job search?"

5b. If the conversation has not been helpful, you should still thank him for his time.

"I want to thank you for taking the time to talk with me."

Whether the telephone interview has been helpful or not, you should write a **thank-you note.**

Scheduling a First Meeting -
The Follow-up Telephone Call after a Letter

1. Introduce yourself, saying a sentence or two about yourself, and ask if he received your letter.

    "My name is Mary Smith; I am graduating from Harvard next June and I am interested in meeting with you to learn about careers in consulting. Did you receive my letter?"

2. If he says that he has received your letter, then continue with a brief explanation of what you are requesting as in item 2 above. The rest of the conversation would proceed in a similar way to the one above.

Answering Machine Etiquette

When your telephone becomes a communication link in your career planning and job search, it is important to realize that the message on your answering machine is part of your representation to employers and career advisers. Whether you are trying to set up an appointment with a career adviser, waiting to hear if you have been selected for interview, or hoping for a job offer, your message creates an impression of you. Make certain that it communicates a sense of competence and professionalism. This means that it should be brief and appropriately worded, and preferably in your own voice. Long musical lead-ins, themes from your favorite television programs, and goofy messages should be avoided. They might cause an employer to hang up without ever leaving that long-awaited message.

SOURCES

Electronic Resume Revolution: Create a Winning Resume for the New World of Job Seeking. Joyce Lain Kennedy and Thomas J. Morrow. John Wiley & Sons, Inc., New York, NY, 1994.
   Describes how to write effective resumes for automated applicant tracking systems; includes samples, as well as a chapter on the video resume interview.

Interview for Success, 4th ed. Caryl Rae Krannich and Ronald L. Krannich. Impact Publications, Manassas Park, VA, 1993.
   Suggestions for making the most of an interview, with chapters on salary negotiation and follow-up. Sample letters and bibliography. Indexed.

Knock 'em Dead: The Ultimate Job Seekers Handbook. Martin Yate. Bob Adams, Inc., Holbrook, MA, 1994.
   Strategies on how to get, survive, and follow up on the interview. Contains a bibliography, a section for disabled job seekers, and an index to sample interview questions.

Sweaty Palms: The Neglected Art of Being Interviewed. H. Anthony Medley. Ten Speed Press, Berkeley, CA, 1992.
   A guide to the entire job-interview process from preparation to follow-up. Covers such topics as how to dress and salary discussions. Appendixes on commonly asked questions, evaluation factors used by interviewers, questions asked by interviewers when they check your references, and questions to ask the interviewer. Bibliography.

Epilogue

Some people let their careers happen by chance. They wait for opportunities to present themselves and take advantage of them as best they can. Others let someone else make decisions for them. They follow the career path that is recommended to them by a parent, a friend, or a teacher.

Some people take charge of their futures and forge their own careers. These individuals seek to understand their own unique interests, values, and abilities. They explore a wide range of possibilities and develop opportunities that enable them to use their talents to make a worthwhile contribution to society. Their careers demonstrate that taking charge of the future and making career choices can be an exciting adventure.

As you undertake career exploration, it is not necessary or desirable to make a lifetime career choice. It may be that the career field that you choose now will be the field that you will work within for the rest of your working life. Or it may be that with time your values and interests will change and you will shift to a different field of work. Careers can be like the digging of a canal: steady progress along a well-defined and predetermined channel. Or they can be like trees growing and developing into unique shapes as they reach for the sun.

To find employment that gives you the opportunity to work towards objectives that you value and challenges you to develop your talents, you need information about yourself: your values, interests, abilities, and goals. You also need information about career fields: the tasks, people, work environments, social impact, and rewards. By integrating information about yourself and about careers, you will be able to set priorities and evaluate options and thus make informed and intelligent choices.

USE OF THE
CAREER BIBLIOGRAPHIES

This appendix is designed as an aid to the use of the many volumes cited in the Sources section at the end of each chapter. The first part is an index of the most important volumes to use as resources for selected career fields; the second is a complete listing of all titles cited in the book. Both indexes indicate the pages on which the pertinent bibliographic information may be found.

Information is given for the following career areas:

Advertising/Public Relations	Manufacturing/Production
Banking/Finance	Marketing/Sales
Consulting	Media/Publishing/Entertainment
Education	Public Interest
Government	Science and Technology
Health/Medicine	Trade/Transportation/Travel
Human Services	Visual and Performing Arts
Law	

The listing for each field includes books that have a chapter or more devoted to that field. Excluded are the more comprehensive descriptive materials that cover virtually the entire range of career options: *The American Almanac of Jobs and Salaries*, the Career Advisor Series, the *Occupational Outlook Handbook*, the VGM Careers for You Series, and the VGM Professional Careers Series, for example. (These are listed in the Career Descriptive Literature section of the bibliography for Chapter 2.) Also excluded from the Appendix listing are professional journals and well-known general indexes such as those to the *Wall Street Journal* and the *New York Times*.

INDEX OF RESOURCES BY CAREER FIELD

Education

Government

Health/Medicine

Manufacturing/Production

Marketing/Sales

Media/Publishing/Entertainment

Trade/Transportation/Travel

Visual and Performing Arts

INDEX OF TITLES

D

E

F

G

H

I

R

S

LIBRARY
ST. LOUIS COMMUNITY COLLEGE
AT FLORISSANT VALLEY.